**Student Evaluation
of Instruction**

Student Evaluation of Instruction

Kenneth O. Doyle, Jr.
University of Minnesota

Lexington Books
D. C. Heath and Company
Lexington, Massachusetts
Toronto   London

Library of Congress Cataloging in Publication Data

Doyle, Kenneth O
    Student evaluation of instruction.

    Bibliography: p. 113
    Includes index.
    1. Student evaluation of teachers. 2. College teachers, Rating
of. I. Title.
LB2333.D69   378.1'2   74–7859
ISBN 0–669–93328–7

Copyright © 1975 by D. C. Heath and Company

Second printing November 1976

Published simultaneously in Canada

Printed in the United States of America

International Standard Book Number: 0–669–93328–7

Library of Congress Catalog Card Number: 74–7859

To My Parents:
Kenneth Owen Doyle
and
Loretta Mayer Doyle

Contents

List of Figures

List of Tables

Foreword

The unexpectedly high attendance at the conferences on student evaluation of teaching held at Temple University and Kansas State University are indication of the need felt by many, many colleges and universities for dependable information about student evaluations. Few individuals are in a better position to fill that need than Ken Doyle. His work at Minnesota has been pioneering. His thoughtful contributions at both conferences were stimulating to me and to other participants. What I particularly like about his approach is his emphasis upon the purposes for which the data are to be used in relationship to validity for these purposes. As his book makes clear, student ratings are not a mechanical device insuring better teaching, but they can be a useful tool for teaching improvement and for other purposes.

When we consider student evaluation as one among a number of tools, it becomes apparent that one needs to ask what information student evaluation can provide, what is the validity of this information as compared with other sources, and what the relative costs and gains of the use of student evaluations may be. Because the number of items and forms is multiplying almost daily, the prospective user needs some conceptualization to guide his or her way. A book of this sort can save months of confusion. Users will find that it can provide a base for continuing development.

Wilbert J. McKeachie

Preface

Ratings are peculiar measures. Most other kinds of educational and psychological devices involve just a person and a task. Achievement tests ask a person to perform the task of answering some questions. Personality inventories and other self-reports ask a person to make some statements about himself. Even projective devices like ink blots involve basically the person and a task. But ratings involve the rater, the task, *and the ratee*—the person or object the rater's task is to describe. The introduction of this third variable makes for a world of difference between ratings and other kinds of measurement. Not only do all the traditional questions about the reliability, validity, and generalizability of data—their precision, meaning, and representativeness—become considerably more complicated, but the standard conceptions of what constitutes good data become themselves ambiguous.

In short, ratings are a complicated form of measurement.

Among these complicated measures, perhaps none is so controversial as student ratings of instruction. The reasons for their controversiality seem both clear and understandable: these ratings constitute at least a perceived threat to the self-esteem, reputation, and job satisfaction of the faculty member, perhaps even a threat to his very career. On the other hand, the pressures on faculty and institution to find ways of documenting instructional effectiveness are tremendous, especially when the educational community as a whole is emphasizing the importance of improving teaching and when fiscal realities are at least reducing growth if not requiring active programs of retrenchment. Thus a tension is created. That most teaching faculty have not had any real training as teachers and are being asked to spend a considerable portion of their professional lives teaching as *their* teachers taught without the confidence that stems from training, and that in many institutions the reward structure continues to favor scholarly productivity over teaching, sometimes in spite of pronouncements and protestations to the contrary—these conditions do nothing to reduce the tension.

Thus arguments abound for and against the use of student ratings as bases for improving teaching, as means for advising students on course selection, and as elements in rank, pay, and tenure decisions. But none of the questions in this debate rings so genuine as the demand to know *How good are these data?* How accurate are they? Are they careless, capricious markings on a sheet of paper, or thoughtful descriptions of the different aspects of the teaching/learning process? What determines the ratings an instructor receives—the actual quality of course and instructor, or factors that have little if anything to do with teaching and the teacher? And other people's ratings, those by colleagues, administrators, even the instructor himself, and other kinds of data, performance measures for example— how well do these compare to student ratings? Finally, what do all these data mean? Can anybody's ratings really say anything at all about who is —and who is not—a good teacher?

So, many of the questions raised about the use of student ratings have really to do with the rigor of the data. This book is largely an examination of the rigor of instructional ratings, student ratings in particular (for much is known, yet much unknown, about these measures), but also colleague, self, and administrator ratings.

In addition, it is an attempt to introduce some organization into a chaotic enterprise, organization that has proven useful in thinking about faculty evaluation, in planning and implementing operating systems, and in interpreting the information that comes from such systems. And it is an exhortation to sensitivity and reasonableness in faculty evaluation, and to concern for rigor of methods and procedures.

It is a book about different roles for different kinds of information, seeking to discover, for a given body of information, whether no weight, or some, or much should be accorded it, and under what conditions. Yet to seek to determine the role of student ratings, and other people's ratings, is not to seek for perfect data. For perfect data, inviolate criteria for effective teaching, simply do not exist. A far more reasonable task, and one chosen for this book, is to try to decide whose ratings, in what fashion used, might help improve educational decisions.

Accordingly, this book is written for the people who need to make educational decisions—faculty, administrators, and students in general— more than for specialists in evaluation and measurement. The difference, though, is one of form not substance. The decision maker's concern, and the psychometrician's, are the same. Only the wording varies. Both groups, then, specialists and nonspecialists as well, might find some useful information here. But each will find frustration too. The decision maker will doubt the need for the apparently self-evident and petty detail and the attempt to formulate a somewhat academic set of criteria for good data; and the psychometrician will cavil at the abuses wrought on timeworn concepts and procedures. But in spite of these deficiencies—or perhaps because of them—the person who makes his way through these pages should find himself at least conversant with the present state of affairs regarding the use of ratings in instructional evaluation.

Many people in different ways have contributed to this book. Though I have met them only through their writings, Professors R. B. Cattell, J. P. Guilford, R. J. Wherry, and Lee J. Cronbach have mightily influenced these pages. Professor Wilbert McKeachie has been a special source of information and encouragement. Professors John Darley, Paul Meehl, David Weiss, and John Feldhusen have made their particular and valued contributions; Susan Whitely, Isaac Bejar, and Darwin Hendel have led me to some most productive insights; and the many friends and colleagues I have met through the Committee on Institutional Cooperation and the Temple, Kansas State, and Manitoba conferences have given more than they received. No less helpful to the production of this book have been Pam Thielke, Marsha Niebuhr, and Mary Strother of the Measurement Services Center, University of Minnesota, and Mike McCarroll, Shirley End, and Darina Williams of D. C. Heath and Co. Finally, for perspective during a most eventful year, to Lynn my wife my gratitude.

Part I
Orientation

1

Conceptualization

The focus of this book is student evaluation of instruction. But before beginning an examination of that rather specific topic, it would be useful to formulate a conceptualization of the whole enterprise of faculty evaluation in order not to lose sight of the facts that instruction is but one of many faculty activities and that students are but one of several sources of evaluative information.

Initial Considerations

A number of topics are essential to any consideration of faculty evaluation, but these five are particularly important during the early stages of the development of a system:

1. the purpose of the evaluation
2. the focus of the evaluation, i.e., the activities or qualities to be evaluated
3. the sources of evaluative information
4. the ways this information can be gathered
5. the technical properties, or quality, of the information

Purposes of Evaluation

Nathan Gage (1958) offered a distinction among kinds of evaluation according to purpose. He noted that teaching can be appraised (a) to provide a basis for *administrative decisions* on academic rank, tenure, and pay; (b) to provide a basis for *self-improvement* on the part of the teachers; and (c) to provide a *criterion for research* on teaching. Other authors (e.g., Werdell, 1967) have suggested a fourth purpose: to provide a basis for *advising students* on course selection. These four are the most often cited reasons for evaluating instructors.

Additional purposes are subsumed under the basic four. Administrative decisions include not only rank, pay, and tenure decisions, but also the *selection* of new faculty from a pool of applicants and the *placement* of

3

faculty—the allocation of faculty time and effort—according to their particular abilities or patterns of effectiveness. Similarly, evaluation to improve faculty performance, besides the improvement of the person as a teacher, can also mean the improvement of the teacher as a person, given that for many people evaluative feedback contributes to personal growth. And evaluation for course or program selection not only involves guiding students into the most appropriate courses but also has ramifications both for modifying courses or programs that appear appropriate for too few students and for changing the composition of the student body to become more commensurate with curricular offerings, by revising course or institutional admissions standards, for example.

The purposes mentioned thus far all focus on the evaluation of faculty in their instructional roles, but all have parallels in the other principal areas of faculty activity. For example, the administrative need for documentation of research effectiveness, whether for the selection, placement, retention, or promotion of faculty, is quite evident. Diagnostic evaluation of research effectiveness can also be useful to faculty who are seeking to enhance their investigative skills. Even evaluation for advising students has something of a parallel in research evaluation, for such evaluation might help graduate students select advisors or mentors whose research strengths seem most likely to satisfy the students' particular tutorial needs. Also, evaluation of research effectiveness can provide a criterion for the study of problems related to the definition of good research and to the teaching of research-related skills and attitudes. (These last two examples illustrate the interaction of teaching, advising, and research.)

It is in some ways necessary and in other ways undesirable to distinguish among purposes. The distinctions are necessary because, for example (as later chapters will argue), the questions to be asked and the rigor demanded of the answers are not necessarily the same for all purposes, nor are the ways the data should be used the same. But these distinctions are at the same time undesirable because they can imply artificial and unintentioned differentiation among faculty improvement, utilization, and reward. Eventually many of these distinctions should blur—but not before better ways of evaluating faculty effectiveness are found.

Focus of Evaluation

One of the principal problems in evaluating faculty effectiveness is the fact that faculty activities are so varied, so individual, so difficult to define. Thus a second essential topic is the definition of faculty activity, the determination of the focus of evaluation.

Faculty are legitimately engaged in many pursuits: teaching and the supervision of teaching; research and the administration of research; advising and counseling; institutional and departmental governance; writing and publishing and other forms of scholarly productivity; fund raising; community service; and so forth. To add to the complexity, these roles are often changing; a faculty member's occupation one term may be very different from that of the previous term, and the change may be in the depth or character of the activity as well as in its name.

While an attempt here to define all faculty activities would likely be fruitless, and while no precise definition even of teaching would find universal acceptance, a descriptive model of teaching may provide an orderly focus for evaluating instruction. Such a model might have three parts: input, process, and outcome. Input in this case means whatever impinges on the senses of the students—what the instructor says and does, what the instructional materials offer (books, syllabi, tests, films, etc.), and what the physical and social environments provide. Process means what the students do—internally—with this stimulation, the various cognitive operations and affective processes they bring to bear on the material. And outcome refers to the products of those processes and operations, that is, the kinds and levels of learning that result.

Input, process, and outcome could also be examined from the instructor's point of view—what he experiences while preparing for and teaching the course, his cognitive and affective responses to that stimulation, and the personal and professional benefits he derives from the experience—but the present attempt to describe teaching needs no additional complication!

Input. Input generally comes from the instructor, the course materials, the students, and the physical environment. The instructor's direct contribution might be separated into scholarly basis (relevant knowledge, choice of goals), presentation (with its communication elements such as clarity and organization as well as its affective components like approachability and positive regard for students), and, perhaps the most important, ability to motivate or stimulate students (Doyle, 1972, and Doyle and Whitely, 1974). Instructional materials can be examined in parallel fashion: their substance and germaneness, their exposition (communication and palatability), and their ability to motivate or stimulate. Anderson and Walberg (in Walberg, 1974) provide a somewhat similar analysis of the social environment, and Kates and Wohlwill (1966) offer some helpful beginnings of a characterization of the physical environment.

Process. What students do with all this stimulation—that is, their *internal* processes—is for the most part beyond the present capabilities of assessment. But, for the sake of completeness, these processes can be described as the activities underlying Bloom's taxonomies of educational objectives (Bloom, 1956; Krathwohl, Bloom, and Masia, 1964): knowing, comprehending, applying, analyzing, synthesizing, evaluating; receiving, responding, valuing, organizing, and characterizing. Guilford (1967) and Guilford and Hoepfner (1966) describe a somewhat similar set of operations: cognition, memory, convergent and divergent thinking, and evaluation.

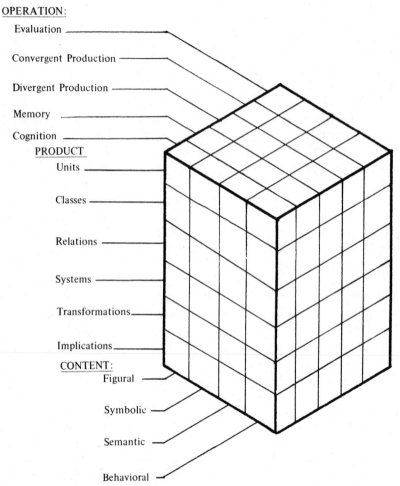

Source: Adapted from Guilford (1968) p. 10. © 1968 by Robert R. Knapp. Reprinted by permission.

Figure 1–1. Guilford's Structure-of-Intellect Model: Intellectual abilities classified in three intersecting ways.

Outcome. The measurement of learning is more within reach than the measurement of mental processes. Guilford writes not only of processes or operations, but also of "contents" and "products." In his formulation, the content of thought can be described as figural, symbolic, semantic, or behavioral; the products of thinking emerge as units, classes, relations, systems, transformations, or implications. A cubic model illustrating this "structure of the intellect" (Figure 1–1) could serve as an admittedly elaborate but useful organizing principle for achievement tests or measures of "outcome." Bloom's efforts bear more directly on classroom testing. The *Handbook on the Formative and Summative Evaluation of Student Learning* (Bloom, Hastings, and Madaus, 1971) includes many illustrations of the use of the taxonomies of educational objectives to construct classroom tests that are in keeping with the purposes of the course. (Later in this chapter, however, some strong reservations will be advanced about the use of classroom tests to evaluate instructors.)

This three-part schema, summarized in Table 1–1, can furnish an outline of instruction upon which an evaluation can be constructed. That is, it can sharpen the focus of an evaluation.

The objection might be raised that this schema assumes the traditional

Table 1–1

A Conceptualization of Instruction

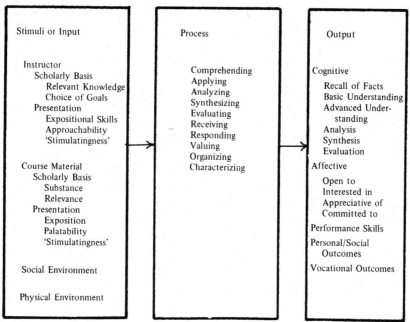

lecture mode of instruction. Not so. The model simply describes the domain of instruction; just as not all courses intend to achieve all of Bloom's objectives, not all courses employ all of these modes of stimulation or input. Seminars, tutorials, independent study, and lecture courses differ from one another in the shifting emphasis each places on the various input sources. (For a useful elaboration of instructor roles in discussion courses and other kinds of courses, see McKeachie, 1969, especially chapters 6–10.)

Sources of Evaluative Data

In brief, the sources of information that can be incorporated into an evaluation are the people who have observed or otherwise experienced one or more of the activities to be evaluated. With regard to the evaluation of instruction, the typical sources of information are the instructor, his present or former students, and at least some of his colleagues. Less typically, other people may be able to provide useful information: administrators, parents and employers of the students, instructional specialists, and so forth.

Ways Information can be Gathered

Evaluation almost reflexively brings to mind questionnaires and rating scales. In addition to these, however, are such important vehicles as letters of commendation, tests (including course examinations and standardized tests), and conversations, dialogues, or verbal reports. While it is probably desirable in evaluations for administrative decisions that all information be in written or tabulated form (to reduce impressionistic judgment, and, especially in case of grievance proceedings or litigation, to provide a reviewable record), evaluations for faculty improvement are not necessarily so restricted in their choice of ways to gather information. Indeed there is an unfortunate tendency to substitute rating scales and other devices for the more flexible and complete communication that written or spoken narratives can provide. Dialogues with the faculty member are especially important because, more than any other type of communication, dialogue can result in clear and complete communication.

This is not to say that rating scales have no place in evaluations for faculty improvement. On the contrary, the strengths of these devices are quite evident: they are economical, readily summarized, and recordable; information gathered with them can be compared to certain other information (a person's earlier ratings, for example, or other people's ratings); rating scale items and data can be studied and refined in such a way that the necessary technical properties of the information are known and the relevant data-quality criteria met; respondents in most instances can be anonymous; and so forth. But, for all these strengths, rating scales remain summary devices that whenever possible should be supplemented by other kinds of information.

Some informational devices are useful for some kinds of evaluation but not for others. For instructional improvement, a show of hands or color-coded cards to indicate confusion or other difficulty can transmit immediate feedback to the instructor. It has been suggested that classrooms could be wired like some legislative chambers—students could have one or more buttons on their desks and could signal the instructor their satisfactions or dissatisfactions, a pattern of lights on the instructor's console advising him continuously of student reaction. Less dramatically, an instructor can watch his students.

Parent, Vaughan, and Wharton (1971) have proposed that instructors meet regularly with a few of their students to discuss and evaluate the course. The volunteer students also serve as ombudsmen or liaisons between the rest of the students and the instructor. The authors recommend this procedure as a supplement to more mechanized evaluations. A variant of this approach is occasionally used, namely having a student ally or colleague attend class and signal the instructor if things are not going well.

Some evaluative information is less useful for faculty improvement than for other kinds of evaluation. The very general or "high inference" rating scale item—e.g., "How would you rate this instructor's over-all teaching ability?"—may be a very good item in terms of technical properties (Doyle and Whitely, 1974), but it provides little in the way of helpful diagnostic information. Such general items are perhaps most useful for administrative decisions, for advising students, and for research.

An extended discussion about the use of classroom examinations and standardized tests for evaluating individual instructors is warranted because of the relatively common proposition that instructors should be judged by their "products," i.e., by what their students learn. Although the proposition itself is in some ways intuitively appealing, its implementation involves logical and practical problems and technical difficulties that render the direct use of student test data for evaluating instructors, in Glass' words, "an egregious error." Glass argues (in Wahlberg, 1974) that standardized tests are designed to uncover gross deficiencies in basic skills, not to reveal the variety of ways teaching can be meaningful, and that such tests give teachers of brighter students an unfair advantage that no statistical machination can effectively eliminate. And, because this use of tests involves some measure of student "gain" during the course, Glass points out the fallibility of test scores of individual students and the compounding of measurement error in the calculation of these so-called "gain scores." (See Harris, 1963, for a compendium of problems in measuring change.) Finally, Glass worries about the consequences of using tests to evaluate instructors:

Teachers would teach the 'safe' topics, possibly at the expense of the elusive but important ones. Teachers would not be permitted to administer their own standardized tests; an expensive external proctoring system would be required, and its costs in terms of trust might even exceed its cost in dollars. [Pp. 12 and 14]

These deficiencies are compounded in college and university settings because (a) standardized tests appropriate for the majority of college courses are unavailable, and so reliance would have to be placed on classroom examinations which are seldom so well constructed as standardized tests; (b) the variety of courses taught in college would make it virtually impossible to compare one instructor's student gains to another's (even if trustworthy "gain scores" could be produced); and (c) the goals of college instruction are probably more varied than in primary and secondary school and less exclusively defineable in terms of achievement test content. Thus Glass's objections apply to postsecondary education with even greater force.

In addition to these technical and administrative problems in the use of tests to evaluate instructors is an important philosophical question that rises with regard to evaluations for administrative decisions: Should instructors be rewarded or punished on the basis of matters that are at least to some extent beyond their control? The abilities and motivation of students and the quality of available instructional materials are examples of circumstances that can vary to increase or diminish an instructor's personal responsibility for student performance and, therefore, the legitimacy of using student performance measures to evaluate him. The less able and motivated an instructor's students, and the less available good instructional materials, the less responsible an instructor would seem to be for student learning. This notion of varying responsibility should by itself be sufficient to persuade one to proceed very cautiously in using student achievement, however measured, to evaluate instructors for administrative purposes. Given the technical and administrative problems already discussed, the reasonable decision would have to be to refrain from using test data for such purposes.

Test data, however, can legitimately make an *indirect* contribution to instructor evaluation by providing data for the partial validation of rating scales and similar devices, that is, by helping evaluators determine which course and instructor characteristics are most likely to result in desirable outcomes for the majority of students and thus to construct more useful rating scales. Test data and other measures of learning can be useful in course improvement evaluations as loose indexes for the instructor of his success in helping students achieve some kinds of goals. Student learning measured by other means than tests (e.g., the "goal-attainment" ratings described in chapter 2) may be able to avoid some of the problems tests encounter, but the use of these measures at least for personnel decisions will probably remain encumbered by the problem of attributing proper responsibility to the instructor.

Quality of Information

The qualities of evaluative information are reliability, validity, generalizability and utility. Reliability deals with precision: How free are the data from error—mechanical errors of scoring and computing as well as measurement errors ranging from the subtle tendency on the part of some raters to mark adjacent items similarly to the more gross errors of carelessness and deliberate falsification? Validity speaks to meaning: What does the information mean? What direct meaning can be drawn from it, and what implications? Generalizability is representativeness: Whose opinions and observations do the data reflect? How well does the sample of information portray the totality of the person's teaching? To what extent do situational factors influence the evaluations? Finally, utility summarizes the situation: What purposes can the data serve?

Information from whatever source, about whatever faculty activity, and gathered in whatever way needs to be evaluated in terms of each of these qualities. Explicit here is the position that some kinds of evaluation require data of higher quality than other kinds. A reasonable ethic in this regard would be that the greater the potential for harm to individuals, the more rigorous the data need to be (Doyle, 1972, *passim;* Guilford, 1954, pp. 388–89). Since neither students nor faculty are likely to be severely and individually harmed by wrong decisions about course presentation and the like, it would seem that course improvement evaluations can proceed with data of lesser rigor than would be required for administrative decisions, in which considerable harm to individual faculty could occur. Chapters 3, 4, 5, and 6 will examine the quality of various kinds of data in terms of the purposes they are to serve.

A Conceptual Schema

These five initial considerations—purposes of evaluation, focus, sources of information, ways of gathering data, and quality of information—can be presented in a five-dimensional schema that defines much of the domain of faculty evaluation and shows the place of student ratings in it. Figure 1–2 is the overall conceptualization. Figure 1–3 is a closer view of one of the cells from the overall schema.

Immediately striking to the eye is the complexity of faculty evaluation.

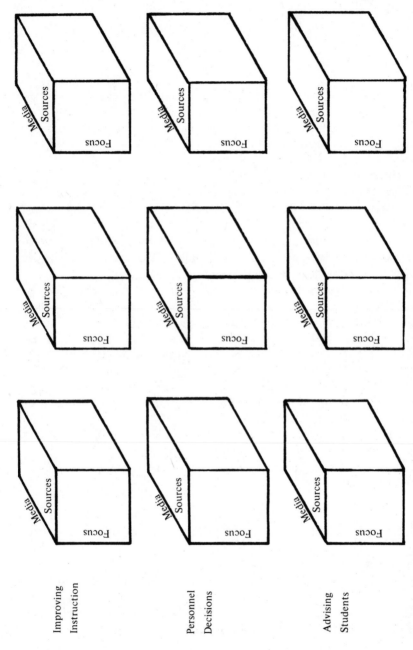

Figure 1–2. A Conceptualization of Instructional Evaluation.

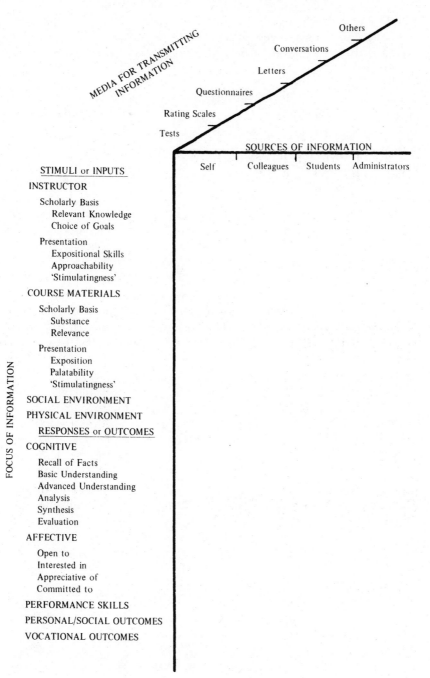

Figure 1–3. One Cube from the Over-all Conceptualization.

Several hundred cells comprise the basic schema, and these cells each generate a host of specific questions.

Also striking is the place of student evaluation of instruction in the total picture. Only a fraction of the cells pertain to instruction, and their number is further reduced when restricted to information from students. Yet these relatively few cells have been sufficient, by virtue of their complexity, importance, and sensitivity, to generate a great deal of research (see reviews and bibliographies by: Meehl, 1941; Wherry, 1952; Morsh and Wilder, 1954; Costin, Greenough, and Menges, 1971; Doyle, 1972; and de Wolf, 1974).

Besides highlighting the dimensions of faculty evaluation and pointing out the place of student evaluations of instruction, a schema such as this can impose a degree of systematization and specification on a generally ambiguous field, and can be used to formulate a variety of questions that require rational or empirical investigation. Few of the specific entries on any of the five dimensions, however, are meant to be unalterable; the purposes and sources especially are open to change as local requirements dictate, and the focus cannot be considered "correct" until further study either confirms these entries or suggests better ones. The most interesting questions raised by this framework are found where the different dimensions intersect. For example, in the leftmost column of cubes in Figure 1–2: what is the comparative reliability of information from the different sources (self, colleagues, students, . . .) gathered in various ways (dialogues, questionnaires, rating scales, . . .) about the different faculty activities? Is the reliability of these data sufficient for the purpose of the evaluation? Similarly, from Figure 1–3: What can each of these groups of people say about each of the faculty activities? How can this information be gathered? As presented here, Figure 1–3 is especially useful in devising evaluation systems; it serves as a kind of evaluation plan seeking sources of information about various activities. Figure 1–2 is more useful as an overview of the field and for evaluating evaluation systems. In the extreme, one could proceed methodically through the entire schema, looking for answers to all of the questions raised, ready to challenge any of the specific entries on the principal axes. More reasonably perhaps, one could pay attention just to those sections that seem most likely to meet the requirements of one's own circumstances.

Subsequent Considerations

There are still other considerations, those that are more important, perhaps, when it comes time to interpret evaluative information.

Moderators

A responsible interpretation of any kind of evaluative data, including student evaluations, requires attention to circumstances that might materially affect the meaning of the information, that might qualify or *moderate* it. Three prominent modifiers are evaluatee responsibility and evaluator competency and motivation. Responsibility has already been mentioned as a reason for caution in using student outcome measures to evaluate instructors; it was argued that an instructor's responsibility for student outcome is diminished by factors beyond his control, and that the appropriateness of using student outcomes for evaluating instructors is correspondingly diminished. In the same vein, other circumstances may affect responsibility. An instructor might receive an unfavorable evaluation with regard to the textbook he uses; but if all the texts in the area are poor, or if the better texts are prohibitively expensive, and if the instructor is aware of these problems, then he cannot be held so responsible for the deficiency as the person who is simply unable to distinguish good materials from bad. Similarly, the junior faculty member who is required to teach material with which he is not familiar and does a poor job is not so responsible as his senior colleague who chooses to teach the material and does it just as poorly.

Evaluator competency to evaluate is another moderator, whether this refers to the competency of colleagues who seldom or never set foot in an instructor's classroom to evaluate his classroom presentation, or the competency of students fully to evaluate the depth and breadth of an instructor's knowledge. It would, of course, be better to avoid this problem by taking pains to see that people are asked to evaluate only those qualities which seem to lie within their powers of assessment (by using Figure 1–3, for example); but circumstances vary, and some degree of attention to evaluator competency is always prudent.

Then there is the question of evaluator motivation. The concern here is not so much the subtle phenomena like the so-called leniency effect in ratings, in which many raters tend to give evaluations that are perhaps a bit too generous, but more the gross motivational phenomena like fear, politics, favoritism, competitive resentment, retaliation, and so forth, whether on the part of students, colleagues, or any other source of information. Unhappily, these qualities are not entirely foreign to academe—or to human nature—and there seems no way to eradicate them, although sometimes the situation provides some guidance. Knowing that two colleagues have a special social or political relationship, whether positive or negative, should suggest caution in the interpretation of one's evaluation of the other. Knowing that an instructor is a controversial figure on campus, or that he teaches a controversial subject, should alert one to the possibility of bias. If the medium is a verbal report or a written narrative, it may be possible to sense the bias from the wording and expression and reduce the weight accorded to that evaluation. If the medium is a rating scale, bias on the part of a relatively few raters will be absorbed in the bulk of the data (especially when averages of a large number of ratings are computed), and positive biases will to some extent cancel out negative ones. If many people are biased in the same direction, that very fact is evaluative of something, and the person who interprets the data will need to understand the situation, gather additional information as necessary, and be ready to modify his interpretation in the light of growing understanding. It will never be possible to eliminate all bias, but truly devastating bias is probably very rare. A person interpreting evaluative data can quite safely proceed under the assumption that the influence of these kinds of bias is slight—unless circumstances dictate otherwise.

Developmental Data

The fact that evaluative information is usually gathered at isolated points in time (e.g., the last week of a term; the end of each year before a tenure decision) raises two problems. First, some care should be taken to ascertain how representative the information is of a faculty member's *typical* effectiveness rather than descriptive of atypically worse or better performance. This problem of representativeness may be larger or smaller, depending on the nature of the information. For example, the report of an extensive research project may contain information evaluative of a researcher's performance over a long period of time. On the other hand, another report might be the result of a weekend's leisurely activity. Student evaluations may present a problem in this regard, not only because of the time-sampled nature of the data (which can be remedied at least to some extent by the simple use of adverbs like "usually") but also because of the possibility that the timing of the evaluation (e.g., immediately before or after examinations versus at an emotionally more neutral point in the term) may to some extent influence the substance of the evaluation. Peer evaluations involve a similar and perhaps greater problem, namely the possible nonrepresentativeness of the occasions of teaching witnessed by the colleague observers.

The second time-related problem in faculty evaluation has to do with evaluations and individual faculty growth. Because information gathered at isolated points in time may lack the context necessary for a meaningful interpretation, evaluation should be a repeated if not continuous undertaking. The most useful evaluative data are those that reveal patterns of effectiveness over time, particularly, perhaps, in the case of younger faculty, or faculty who have experienced, say, a rebirth of interest in teaching. The more likely a person is to be changing, the more important it is that evaluations be able to reflect the change.

Consequences of Evaluation

A thorough utilization of evaluative information will include attention to the possible consequences of the evaluation. One type of consequence (resentment, retaliation) has already been suggested in the discussion of evaluator motivation. But other more subtle consequences may be involved. To give some examples, an uncomplimentary evaluation could certainly hurt the career development of a young untenured faculty member, but it could also enhance his development if it contributed to some adaptive change of behavior or if it guided—or forced—him into circumstances in which he was more likely to be both satisfied and satisfactory. A complimentary evaluation, on the other hand, could confirm or improve a faculty member's status and remuneration. But it could also excite the envy of his colleagues, which could ultimately be more harmful to him than an unfavorable evaluation might have been. A favorable evaluation of teaching could, paradoxically, lead a chairman to urge a person, say, who loved research and who also happened to be a good teacher to increase his teaching load at the expense of time for research. A favorable evaluation might result in a special cash award for being an effective teacher; but if the receipt of this award operates against the instructor's chances for a routine cost-of-living raise, then the reward, over the long run, becomes a punishment.

These examples, though they scarcely exhaust the possibilities, should be sufficient to express the caution that the consequences of evaluation can be many and varied—and sometimes quite unintended.

Institutional Goals

The final set of considerations affecting the interpretation of evaluative information has to do with the goals of the institution. Evaluations need to be considered in the light of institutional goals. In a school with a primarily instructional emphasis, it matters less that a person be a good researcher than that he be a good teacher. In a research institute, the faculty member's teaching is of less concern than his research. In land-grant institutions, the public service role is perhaps more prominent than in private colleges. Generally, the more in keeping with institutional goals is a particular faculty activity, the more weight should be placed on the evaluation of that activity. But in complex institutions with a diversity of goals, this principle can be difficult to apply, at least in the evaluation of individual faculty. Thus some institutions acknowledge a number of legitimate goals, and ask only that their faculty be dedicated to certain ones: teaching or research plus community service or university governance, for example. Perhaps an even better means to serve the same diversity is the so-called Faculty Performance Agreement, a kind of negotiated contract between the institution and the faculty member to the effect that during a specified period of time (a term, a year, a biennium) he will be responsible for a particular set of activities and will be evaluated in terms of his performance of those activities. Thus misunderstandings about responsibilities are avoided, and the framework for an evaluation is agreed upon. Some such agreements specify the weights to be attached to each activity; some even indicate criteria for various levels of performance. How elaborate these agreements should be depends in large measure upon the history and nature of the institution, on the character of the work to be done, and on legal considerations regarding the contractual force of the agreements. But the idea in general has much to recommend it.

These considerations are all essential to a thorough and responsible program for evaluating faculty effectiveness. Some apply mostly during the development of a system and the gathering of data, others are more important when information is to be interpreted and used. All can help guide the evaluation of evaluation programs.

With the perspective provided by this overview of faculty evaluation, subsequent chapters will focus on student evaluation of instruction.

2 Instrumentation

The first reported instance in North America of students rating teachers apparently took place in Sioux City before the turn of the century (Kratz, 1896). Since then, a considerable variety of evaluation systems have developed. Integral to most systems is the "instrument," the questionnaire or rating scale by means of which student opinions and observations are collected. A number of different kinds of instruments can be distinguished by examining the content of the questions, the format of the questions, and the flexibility of the questionnaire itself.

Content of Questions

Either or both of two broad kinds of evaluative questions are found in most evaluation instruments. The first kind asks for student reaction to instructor traits or behaviors, to the various characteristics of the course materials, and to the social and physical environments. For example:

How would you rate this instructor's general teaching ability?

The instructor was approachable.

The instructor talked too fast.

Were the examinations fair?

In your own words, please comment on the usefulness of the outside reading.

The second kind of question in terms of item content focuses on student outcomes, including the amount of progress made toward general or specific educational goals:

How much would you say you learned from this instructor?

Did this course help you develop your creative potential?

To what extent did the problem sets help you to think critically?

How was this course beneficial to you?

Some reservation about the use of student-outcome measures for evaluating instructors was expressed in the earlier discussion of instructor responsibility, concluding with the caution that if ratings of this sort are used care must be taken that the data be qualified in terms of the instructor's personal responsibility for these outcomes. Student-outcome measures remain appealing to many people, however. If the responsibility caveat is observed, it may be that an instrument including outcome ratings as well as trait ratings could be a useful tool (see Hoyt, 1973, and Hoyt, in Sockloff, 1973, for a description of such an instrument, and see Appendix for a copy of the instrument).

A third kind of question appears on many instruments. These questions request personal or demographic information about the respondent (major, sex, year in school, etc.). In themselves, of course, such questions are not evaluative, but they do permit sometimes useful cross tabulations of responses. For example, an instructor teaching a large heterogeneous class might profit from knowing if underclassmen perceive him in the same way as upperclassmen do, or majors the same as nonmajors. These items simply provide the capacity for cross tabulations of this sort.

Format of Questions

Whether of outcomes or of traits, questions can be framed in a number of different ways, the most popular of which are open-ended questions and ratings. Open-ended questions call for prose responses ranging from one word to as many as the student cares to write:

In what special ways has this course contributed to your education?

What I liked most about this course was:

The class discussions:

The importance of open-ended questions in themselves and as supplements to ratings was emphasized in chapter 1. Only dialogue can provide more complete information. Their principal disadvantages are that the responses cannot readily be tabulated, summarized, absorbed, or normed, nor can the information be efficiently studied for its technical qualities.

Ratings can be tabulated and studied. Ratings are multiple-choice questions for which the response options describe judgments or observations about a trait, behavior, or outcome. Because of their extreme popularity, ratings warrant extended treatment here.

Ratings are composed of scales, stems, and cues or anchors. The scale provides the response mode; it is usually numerical, graphical, or pictorial. True/false, yes/no, and agree/disagree questions, as well as checklists, are special two-response cases of numerical scales.

In heavily automated systems, the response generally involves blackening a circle, rectangle, or oblong; less automated systems use circling, checking, underlining, etc. There is no inherent advantage of one scale type over another, except possibly for the somewhat greater work that can be involved in scoring graphical scales. On the other hand, graphical scales permit as fine discriminations as the raters can give and can eliminate the problem of raters wanting to respond part way between presented alternatives. Some raters may find pictorial scales—e.g., little smiling or frowning faces—a bit puerile for their tastes.

The stem of a rating poses the question. It can be very simple or quite detailed:

The instructor was approachable.

Students should receive 45 minutes of instruction during every class period. An appropriate story, personal experience, or joke may illustrate or emphasize a point, while irrelevant stories and discussion waste time. How often did this instructor waste class time with irrelevant discussion (Adapted from Kent, 1966)?

Guilford (1954, p. 296) suggests some rules concerning the formulation of stems. Among his rules are:

1. They should be phrased univocally, objectively, and specifically.
2. They should not be a composite of independent traits, qualities, or behaviors.
3. Each should refer to a single type of activity or to results of a single type of activity.
4. They should be based on past or present accomplishment rather than on what the raters see as future promise.

Berdie and Anderson (1974) provide a more extended discussion of question phrasing, generally complementary to Guilford's.

Cues or anchors define points on the scale. They are usually terse adverbs or adjectives or adverbial or adjectival phrases, although sometimes rather lengthy sentences or vignettes are found. In pictorial scales, the illustrations themselves serve as cues. Guilford (1954, p. 293) suggests some editorial requirements for good cues:

1. *Clarity.* Short statements. Simple, unambiguous terminology.
2. *Relevance.* Consistency with the stem.
3. *Precision.* Reference to an exact point (or very narrow range) on the scale, and unequivocal rank position among other cues.
4. *Variety.* Diversity of language among cues for the same stem, to sharpen differentiation.
5. *Objectivity.* Avoidance (if possible) of terminology implying moral, ethical, or social evaluations.
6. *Uniqueness.* Cues for each stem unique to that stem.

Editing alone, however, is not sufficient. Empirical investigations should be undertaken to determine the psychological distance between pairs of ordered cues—the distance between each pair of scale points should reflect the same quality, quantity, or frequency of the trait or outcome—and to find how wide range of cues is necessary for a particular kind of rating. (See, for example, Bass, Cascio, and O'Connor, 1974.)

Decisions in the Construction of Rating Scales

Some quite specific questions about the construction of rating scales are frequently asked. One common question is, how many scale points should there be? The most frequently employed number of scale points in student ratings (except for continuous graphical ratings, which have an infinity of points) seems to be either four or five, a number apparently borrowed from multiple-choice tests and confirmed by the five-point scoring capability of many test scoring machines. In general, however, the more scale points the better, because the more distinctions raters are allowed to make, the sharper their ratings will be. Good, workable scales of as many as 25 points have been constructed (e.g., Wherry, 1952). But increases in the sharpness (reliability) of the ratings become less and less as the number of scale points is extended beyond about seven; and using many scale points, unless they have been anchored with exceptional care, can irritate and confuse the rater. At the other extreme, scales with four or fewer points, or perhaps even five, may be too restrictive. Many raters tend to avoid the extreme points on a scale, and a five-point scale minus its two extremes leaves only three working points, probably a number insufficient for maximum effectiveness. Although the best number of points for a particular scale is an empirical question, a suggested number for typical situations is six or seven in the case of bipolar or two-directional scales like:

Very Strongly Agree	Strongly Agree	Somewhat Agree	Somewhat Disagree	Strongly Disagree	Very Strongly Disagree

and four or five in the case of unipolar or one-directional scales:

None	Some	Quite a Bit	Very Much	Very, Very Much

The decision between an odd or an even number of scale points depends on two considerations. The first has to do with the tendency of many students to be a bit generous with their ratings. This tendency for ratings to pile up at the more favorable end of the scale reduces the scale's ability to distinguish among the many faculty who receive the higher ratings. One additional scale point at the favorable end can markedly reduce this problem and result in a more useful spread of ratings:

Considerably Below Average	Quite a Bit Below Average	A Bit Below Average	A Bit Above Average	Quite a Bit Above Average	Considerably Above Average	A Great Deal Above Average

There is nothing inherently wrong with an asymetrical scale such as this one, so long as there are at least a sufficient number of both favorable and unfavorable alternatives.

The second consideration, which applies only to bipolar scales, is whether or not one wants a neutral midpoint, like "undecided." In general, neutral midpoints should probably not be used, since they can tempt the raters to be less discriminating than they might otherwise be, to cop out, suspend judgment, and declare themselves neutral or undecided. The absence of a neutral point will often force a little more thought and result in ratings that are correspondingly more precise. (Although not infrequently used, "Does not apply" is rarely an appropriate midpoint—or *scale* point, for that matter—because it interrupts the continuity of most scales. In the ideal situation, all scales should be applicable; more realistically perhaps, raters should be instructed to skip over or strike out inapplicable questions.)

Other frequent questions have to do with the ordering of anchors and the negative phrasing of stems. Some researchers recommend trying to keep the raters attentive by alternating the layout of the instrument so that the complimentary anchor is sometimes first, other times last, and by including negatively phrased stems among the positive. Otherwise, the argument goes, raters will be more influenced by the physical arrangement of the scales than by their content. But varying the direction of the scales seems likely to create more problems than it resolves. The rater who is moving rapidly through the instrument (as raters usually do) can easily miss the change of direction. The error in this case could be considerable because the point the rater selects may be entirely contrary to the point he intended. Negatively phrased stems can cause the same problem, and, in addition, can result in evaluations that are difficult to interpret: "I disagree that the instructor was not fair." Efforts like these give the impression of trying to trick the rater and seem less constructive than putting the same amount of effort into the construction of good rating scales and clear directions.

Variants of Rating Scales

A number of researchers have been experimenting with variants of the traditional rating scale. One such variant involves a double-scale format designed to gather more information, usually qualifying information, than one could gather with any single scale. Gagné and associates at the University of Quebec have developed a double-scale format in which the first scale asks the students to rate the instructor as they actually perceive him, the second scale as they would want him to be. The difference between the two scores is an index of student satisfaction or dissatisfaction. Summary reports suggest that these scales are dependable and are doing what is expected of them (Gagné and Allaire, 1974; see also Levinthal, Lansky, and Andrews, 1971).

A second double-scale strategy has been in operation at the University of Minnesota for several years. The basic scale calls for a trait rating, the second scale for a rating of how important the rater considers that trait (see Appendix). The rated importance of the trait thus accords more or less weight to the interpretation of the trait rating. Some experts argue that it would be more efficient to study item characteristics beforehand and put into the instrument only those that most people consider important or that have demonstrated their importance in other ways (e.g., broad representation of traits or correlations with student-outcome measures). Others claim that measures of the importance of a trait are highly variable and should be obtained from every rater during each evaluation. Many instructors have indicated a preference for such a double-scale arrangement. Crittenden and Norr (1973) found that specific trait ratings weighted by importance ratings are better predictors of over-all evaluations than are unweighted trait ratings, but little other information on the technical aspects of these supplemental data is available.

A rather different kind of double-scale rating system is intuitively appealing but does not seem to be in operation in any faculty evaluation program. This is an approach that grows out of Murray's notion of personal need/environmental press. (Murray, 1938; see also Stern, 1963, Pace, 1963, Astin and Holland, 1961, Betz, Klingensmith, and Menne, 1970, and Dawis, Lofquist, and Weiss, 1968). The process calls for a profile measure of each student's instructional needs (e.g., through self ratings) and a parallel description of what the course offers relative to the satisfaction of each of those needs. Correspondence between a student's "needs" profile and the course's "satisfiers" profile describes the optimal learning situation. If the important need/satisfier dimensions can be identified, this approach may be very useful for improving instruction and advising, but perhaps less so for personnel decisions. (See chapter 4 for elaboration of this needs/satisfiers model.)

Special Attempts to Reduce Ratings Error

Whether gathered by means of these experimental methods or the more traditional approach, all ratings will contain some amount of measurement error. Two examples of measurement error are the so-called halo and leniency effects. Halo effect is the tendency on the part of any rater to let his ratings of specific course or instructor qualities or outcomes be influenced by his over-all impression of the experience. Because of its blurring effect on specific ratings, the halo effect diminishes the diagnostic capability of information and is perhaps more of a problem for course improvement evaluations than for other kinds. Leniency effect refers to the tendency of raters to be a bit too generous in their evaluations, to give the ratee too much of the benefit of the doubt. Leniency can be a problem in almost any kind of evaluation.

Efforts to reduce measurement error have involved sometimes considerable departures from traditional scale format. Two of these departures are the method of scaled expectations and forced-choice ratings.

The principle underlying the method of scaled expectations is that most rating errors are not due to deliberate failings on the part of the raters but rather to poorly constructed, ambiguous scales. Better ratings, the proponents of this method argue, can be obtained by asking questions which the rater can honestly answer about behaviors he can observe (Smith and Kendall, in Barnette, 1968). Construction of scales of this sort usually involves gathering "critical incidents" or descriptive examples of better and worse instructor behavior from people representative of those who will ultimately use the scales. Each of these descriptions or incidents is then rated in terms of how good or bad it seems. These ratings are used to arrange the critical incidents (which now become behavioral anchors) on a graphical continuum. These scales are widely used in industry for personnel evaluation but do not yet seem to have found their way into education.

Several authors have suggested the technical superiority of scales of this sort (e.g., Smith and Kendall, 1963; Dunnette, 1966; Campbell, Dunnette, Arvey, and Hellervik, 1973), although other studies have failed to find a distinct advantage to these scales over more traditional ones (Burnaska and Hollman, 1974; Borman and Vallon, 1974). While it may be that the effort that goes into the construction of behavioral expectation scales would improve any rating format, experimentation with behavioral expectation scales in an educational context seems called for.

Another kind of scale devised to counter measurement error in ratings is the forced-choice scale, of which there are a number of variants (see Berkshire and Highland, 1953, for a comparison of six forced-choice techniques). The essential feature of these scales is that they require the rater to choose among equally desirable alternatives, only some of which describe effective instructors. These scales often consist of four descriptive phrases or cues that have been found to be of equal attractiveness or "social desirability," but only two of which empirically distinguish perceived effective from perceived ineffective instructors. For example:

Is able to explain concepts in more than one way.

Never showed favoritism.

Organized discussions logically.

Referred to the text when uncertain about a question.

The rater's task is to choose the two items that are most descriptive of the ratee. The instructor's score is the total number of *discriminating* items checked across all sets of items. For a more complete description of how to construct forced-choice scales and a discussion of the theory that underlies them, see Wherry (1952), Berkshire and Highland (1953), Guilford (1954), and Sharon (1970).

Several studies have found these scales more resistant to measurement error than other kinds of scales: Baier (1952), Taylor and Wherry (1951), and Berkshire and Highland (1953). Especially persuasive are reports by Sharon (1970; see also Sharon and Bartlett, 1969) and by Wherry (1952). Sharon constructed a forced-choice scale and a graphical scale with the same content and asked beginning psychology students to rate their instructors. He told some of the students that the ratings were for research purposes only and could be completed anonymously (control condition); others he told that the ratings would go to a faculty committee charged with evaluating the instructors (evaluation condition); still other students were asked to sign the rating forms (identification); and a final group were told they would be asked to explain the ratings to the instructors face to face (justification). The forced-choice ratings did not differ across the four conditions, but the graphic ratings were significantly more favorable from evaluation and justification students than under the control condition. Furthermore, the graphic ratings all showed some leniency effect while the forced-choice ratings did not.

Wherry, an early proponent of the forced-choice technique, tested forced-choice scales, graphic scales, and a checklist against measures of student learning (course examination scores adjusted for ability). Only the forced-choice scales correlated positively and significantly with this measure of learning. (But see chapter 4 for some tempering comments on validity studies of this sort.)

Other authors, however, have criticized forced-choice methodologies for presenting a difficult and annoying task to the raters, for being inordinately difficult to devise, and for not consistently producing the results claimed by the original developers (Travers, 1951; Guilford, 1954; and Nunnally, 1967).

A further problem with the use of forced-choice scales for evaluating instruction is that the ratings cannot be used diagnostically. They furnish only a single-score summary, with no indication of the stronger and weaker aspects of the instructor's performance. In addition, the method of analysis forces one to accept the scale builder's definition of good teaching; it does not allow one to weight some instructor characteristics more or less than others. These problems may not be unresolvable, however. Researchers at the University of Minnesota (see Gay, Weiss, Hendel, Lofquist, and Dawis, 1971) have developed a kind of diagnostic forced-choice scale for the Minnesota Importance Questionnaire (a measure of vocational needs). It may also be possible to construct sets of forced-choice items *within* categories of instructor behavior, so that scoring these sets separately would provide a diagnostic capability. One might also consider devising a forced-choice scale intended primarily for administrative decisions but supplemented by more traditional scales and/or open-ended questions for diagnostic purposes. The forced-choice scale deserves another round of rigorous consideration.

All things considered, the conclusion must be that there is no perfect question format or scaling methodology. All ratings are and will continue to be influenced by some amount of measurement error. This is not to say that the error is crippling, only that the precision of the information—and therefore its utility—is to some extent diminished (see chapters 3 and 6). The search for ways to increase this precision will go on. As it does, it should involve not only attempts to improve scaling methodology and question formats, but also efforts to train and motivate the raters.

Flexibility of Instruments

Many institutions have tried to develop a single questionnaire or rating scale for use in all courses. Not surprisingly, these instruments have often been criticized by faculty and students as irrelevant to the specific needs of particular courses. The wrong questions are asked, the critics say, and important questions excluded. Although the criticism is sometimes invalid, simply a manifestation of resistance or egocentrism, it is frequently legitimate and has led to attempts to devise more flexible instruments.

One relatively simple way to increase flexibility is to leave room on the questionnaire for an instructor to add his own items. This is often done by appending to the basic instrument a number of scales, just the response grids, without stems or anchors (see Appendix). The instructor can write his own stems and anchors on the blackboard or mimeograph them on a separate sheet of paper, and the students can respond on the preprinted response grids. These supplementary data can be processed just like the data from the standard items. This approach can assure that no important questions are omitted, but it cannot, of course, remove any undesired items from the basic questionnaire.

A second effort to resolve the relevancy problem has been the module approach, that is, the construction of different questionnaires for different specific purposes. Modules have appeared titled Tests and Grading, Reading Materials, The Instructor, The Teaching Assistant, Laboratories, Recitations, Seminars, Audio/Visual Materials and Procedures, and so forth. Faculty are invited to choose the modules most appropriate to their particular courses. Princeton University, University of Quebec, Western Washington State College, and the University of Minnesota are among the schools that have experimented with such modules (see Appendix).

Still more flexibility is provided by the computer-based "cafeteria" system originated by Derry and associates at Purdue University (Derry et al., 1974; see also Starry, Derry, and Wright, 1973) and similar though less technology-oriented procedures developed by Whitney at the University of Iowa and Turner at Indiana University (personal communication). In Derry's system, instructors are provided a catalogue of rating items from which they select the items they prefer. They mark the preferences on a machine-readable order blank, and the order is read into the system. A computer line printer immediately prints as many copies of the tailor-made questionnaire as the instructor requests. Provisions in the system allow departments and colleges and the university itself to specify sets of core items to be printed on the questionnaires of all their faculty, partly to permit more penetrating research on sets of standard items and partly to preclude instructors' devising questionnaires that tap only their strong points. The questionnaires are machine readable, and an elaborate system of data recall (for norms) and computerized storage has been devised. The Whitney and Turner systems are analogous to Derry's except that the computer directs an on-line typewriter to prepare a master copy of the tailored questionnaire, and a separate offset printer duplicates the copies onto preprinted machine-readable answer sheets. Photocopying machines on special pricing plans may be more cost/effective for many institutions. Data processing (at least so far) is not so elaborate as with the Purdue system.

A somewhat similar but more rudimentary (and correspondingly inexpensive) version of the cafeteria approach has been used by some individual faculty at the University of Minnesota. They have prepared a collection of rating items that they consider appropriate to at least some of their courses and have typed those items on narrow strips of heavy paper (card stock). When they want to evaluate a particular course, they select the items they want, arrange the paper strips on a photocopier, and duplicate the number of questionnaires needed. This approach was developed purely for their personal convenience and does not include the sophisticated data processing of the grander systems nor the control of externally specified sets of core items.

Even when instructors have complete freedom to select evaluation items, complaints can still be heard, this time from students who sometimes object to the content of the questionnaire. Kiresuk at the Program Evaluation Project at Hennepin County General Hospital in Minneapolis has devised a system that allows almost complete *rater* choice of questionnaire content (Kiresuk and Sherman, 1968). Although this work is geared toward the evaluation of psychotherapy by patients, the methodology should transfer quite easily to student evaluation of instruction. In Kiresuk's system of "goal-attainment scaling," the patient, before therapy begins and with the help of an intake interviewer or a programmed text, constructs a list of his major symptoms or problems and creates a kind of behavioral-expectation rating scale to measure progress toward the resolution of each problem. At the same time, the patient indicates his current status with respect to each goal and weights each problem in terms of its importance to him. At various stages during the therapeutic experience and afterwards (including a follow-up six months or a year later), the patient again indicates his status. Progress or regression with regard to the various goals, moderated by the rated importance of each goal, defines the patient's goal-attainment score which, taken across many patients, becomes an index of the therapist's effectiveness.

For the evaluation of instruction, the self-stated educational goals of the individual students would substitute for the therapeutic goals of Kiresuk's patients. The rest of the procedure could remain basically the same. The system is intriguing for its potential in diagnostic evaluations and possibly for course selection, although some changes in the analysis would be necessary to provide profiles of more and less successful goal attainment. Because it is based upon outcomes that are not entirely under the instructor's control, and because it contains no satisfactory way to distinguish easily achieved goals from more difficult ones, the use of goal-attainment scaling for administrative decisions should be undertaken very cautiously, if at all.

Comparing these diverse approaches to one another, it seems clear that the single-instrument approach is certainly the simplest, both conceptually and logistically. It has another advantage as well: it permits the commitment of relatively more research to questionnaire construction and development and is therefore likely to produce a technically superior instrument. But the need for consumer acceptance remains, and a technically superior instrument is of little use if students refuse to complete it and faculty and administrators refuse to consider it. Some greater acceptance of standard questionnaires can be achieved by means of supplementary items provided by individual instructors. The reliability and validity of these supplementary items can only be assumed, however.

At the other extreme, Kiresuk's scoring formula is mathematically sound, but the final scores depend on the goodness of the data that are entered into the equation, and until the reliability of the individual's sequential ratings has been demonstrated, as well as the reliability of the goal weightings, the system must be considered experimental. Trying to adapt the system to an educational setting may be difficult too, for it would not only require considerable cooperation on the part of students and faculty for the initial goal-setting and repeated progress ratings, but, especially in larger institutions, it could create major data storage and retrieval problems, since subsequent ratings need to be compared to prior ones. Its problems notwithstanding, the possibility that this approach could foster greater goalorientedness in students and faculty is itself enough to commend it to further study.

The modular approach and the cafeteria systems appear to offer many advantages and relatively few disadvantages. Both offer what seems to be at least a reasonable amount of flexibility. The modules themselves and the core items in the cafeteria are amenable to extensive research, although the multiplication of instruments (including core-item sets) probably means that research resources would have to be spread thinner over a wider range of tasks. The modules reduce but do not eliminate complaints from consumers; the cafeteria, on the other hand, may be more expensive to install and operate. If the cafeteria system or some variation can be made cost effective in a given institution, and if the items available for selection are pre-screened for basic psychometric quality, the cafeteria approach or some variant may be the most desirable choice.

The principal considerations in the selection of any evaluation system are the technical strength of the data, cost, and acceptance by consumers. The choice of one system over another will have to depend in large measure on an institution's own assessments of its particular needs, resources, and commitment to evaluation. The next three chapters will appraise the quality of the data.

Part II
Quality

3 Reliability

Reliability means precision. In educational and psychological measurement, perfect reliability—perfect precision—is never achieved. The proper question, then, is not whether data are perfectly precise, but whether they are precise enough and of the right kind of precision to serve a particular purpose.

In chapter 1 an ethic was proposed, namely that information needs to be more precise, the more *harm to individuals* there could accrue from its use. This is a judgmental matter, certainly; but many would agree with the proposition that more serious harm could befall individuals if personnel decisions were made on the basis of imprecise data than if decisions, say, to change the format of a course or style of presentation were made with similarly imprecise information. Consequently, the greatest degree of reliability should be required of information intended to influence personnel decisions.

This chapter will review the technical literature on the reliability of student ratings of instruction in an attempt to reach some conclusions about the adequacy of this information to serve the purpose intended of it. For the sake of perspective, the reliability of student ratings will whenever possible be compared to the reliability of data from other sources—colleagues, administrators, and the instructor himself.

A reasonably thorough review must begin with a reasonably thorough explication of the meaning of reliability. Reliability does mean precision. But, like heat, reliability is perhaps better understood in terms of its opposite. What, then, can subtract from the precision of information?

One source of imprecision is computational error: errors of tabulation or errors of arithmetic, errors of keypunching or optical scanning, even errors like putting the wrong instructor's name on a ratings summary! These errors will be assumed absent or corrected.

A second source of error is the rater's task itself. To the extent that he has lacked the opportunity to observe what he is asked to rate, to the extent that the question he is asked to answer is ambiguous or offensive or irrelevant, the rater's answers may lose precision. And to the extent that the question does not allow the respondent to use his full powers of discrimination, the potential for reliability will not be achieved. A considerable body of research exists on these and related topics and will be examined in the following pages.

Another source is the environment. Lighting, ventilation, and general comfort in the rating situation could conceivably affect ratings, as could the social milieu at the time of or immediately before the rating. The physical environment seems unlikely to have any great bearing on student ratings of instruction, but the impact of the social circumstances surrounding the rating situation could have considerable impact. Unfortunately there seems to have been little if any student ratings research on this latter potential source of unreliability (but see Schachter, in Glass, 1967, for an example of social influence on ratings of another kind).

A fourth source of error is the rater. If his memory of the ratee is dimmed or if he lacked the skill or motivation to observe or lacks the capability of drawing his memories together perceptively or is simply thoughtless or careless or tired or in an especially good or bad mood, the reliability of his ratings may suffer. (If he is malicious, however, his ratings may or may not be reliable, depending on the particular measure of reliability and the cleverness of the malicious expression. Hence the caution expressed in chapter 1 about rater motivation.)

Especially when the task is ambiguous and the rater deficient in skill and motivation, certain subtle forms of rating error can arise. Two of these have already been discussed, halo and leniency error. In addition to these are:

Central Tendency—the inclination to rate toward the midpoint of a scale, especially on bipolar scales

Proximity Error—the tendency to rate adjacent items similarly

Logical Error—rating items similarly because the traits they represent "ought" to go together

Contrast Error—the projection of one's own deficiencies onto the ratee

Several of these have their converse errors: the tendency to choose the extremes of a scale, to mark adjacent items dissimilarly ("sharpening"), and to overrate a person's strengths in terms of one's own weaknesses.

Three final kinds of error depend on the prior experience of the rater: implicit theories, or preconceptions of a person's behavior patterns based on one's accumulated experience with previous instructors or people in general; expectations, similar to but broader than implicit theories, and involving rumors and reputations as well as prior experience; and first impressions, anticipations that an instructor will continue to behave in keeping with the rater's initial perception of him.

Some of these errors are considered random because their presence and direction in a person or a group are essentially unpredictable: careless reading of items, accidental mismarking of the rating scale, momentarily flagging motivation, and so forth. Others are thought of as constant or systematic because they occur in the same person consistently or consistently in many or all students in a class. Random errors are more easily assessed and corrected than systematic errors.

A number of different ways of measuring the extent of random error have been devised. The standard methods come under the headings of internal consistency or homogeneity and retest reliability or stability. Internal consistency [a] is an index of content similarity, agreement across items (see Cattell, 1964). If all items in a set measure the same thing, i.e., correlate highly, the set is said to be internally consistent, and the rating a person gives on one item is predictable from his ratings on the other items. The more random error there is in ratings with that set of items, the lower will be the internal consistency.

But contrary to common practice, internal consistency is an appropriate quality of an item set only to the extent that the items *should* be measuring the same thing. For example, the first of the following sets of items should be more internally consistent than the second:

Clearly presented the subject matter
Made good use of examples and illustrations
Communicated well

Clearly presented the subject matter
Was friendly
Stimulated me to think

Thus, simply computing the internal consistency of an entire questionnaire would be inappropriate unless the whole instrument were intended to measure a single quality and produce a single summary score across all items. The items should be logically or empirically clustered and the statistic applied to each cluster. Cluster scores could then be reported, qualified by their respective reliabilities.

A considerable number of published studies have included measures of internal consistency, and most professionally constructed questionnaires employ internal consistency measures somewhere in their development. Table 3–1 summarizes some of these applications. The degree of freedom from random error indicated by these studies compares quite favorably with the reliability of well constructed commercially published achievement tests. For this reason, and because increasing the internal consistency of a set of

---

[a] Internal consistency is measured by a variety of statistics: Coefficient Alpha (Cronbach, 1951); the Kuder-Richardson formulas (Kuder and Richardson, 1937); the Hoyt (1941) and Horst (1949) procedures, and others (see Thorndike, in Jackson and Messick, 1967). Terms like "odd-even," "split-half," "random pairs," and "random groups of items" are signals that internal consistency is being measured.

Table 3–1

Illustrative Studies of the Internal Consistency of Student Ratings of Instructors

Study	Student Sample	Number and Kind of Items	Statistical Formula	Internal Consistency
Wherry (1951)	42	12-item 25-point ratings	Split-half	.88
	46 ⎫ rating past	140-item 25-point ratings	Split-half	.95
	46 ⎬ better and worse instruc-	140-item five-point ratings	Split-half	.96
	47 ⎪ tors	12-item five-point ratings	Split-half	.98
	44 ⎭	70 forced-choice dyads	Kuder-Richardson 14	.88
Lovell and Haner (1955)	105 in 4 courses	36 forced-choice tetrads	Odd-even means	.79 corrected to .88
Remmers and Weisbrodt (1965)	1908 in 59 courses	11 ten-point ratings (PRSI[a])	Horst	.67–.91
Aleamoni and Spencer (1973)	297 regardless of courses	50 five-point ratings (CEQ[b])	Split-half (negative versus positive items)	.85 corrected to .92
		50 five-point ratings	Split-half (mixed negative and positive)	.87 corrected to .93
	? in 16 courses	50-five-point ratings	Kuder-Richardson 21	.93 average
Hildebrand, Wilson, and Dienst (1971)	94–571 in 7 courses	8–10 item CEQ[b] subscales	Kuder-Richardson 21	.40–.92
	1015 rating past best and worst instructors	7–8 item seven-point ratings	Alpha	.80–.89
Doyle (1972)	379 in 11 courses	9–28 item 5-point ratings (SOS[c])	Hoyt	.90–.96
	379 in 11 courses	2–6 item 5-point ratings (SOS[c])	Hoyt	.61–.92

[a] Purdue *Rating Scale for Instructors*
[b] Illinois *Course Evaluation Questionnaire*
[c] Minnesota *Student Opinion Survey*

items is not an especially difficult matter,[b] it seems safe to conclude that student ratings are—or, in the very least, can be made to be—very reliable in the sense of internal consistency. It should be noted, however, that when concise subscales of a few items are constructed from a more general questionnaire, the internal consistency of these subscales may drop markedly, largely because of the lesser number of items (e.g., Aleamoni and Spencer, 1973 and 1970, and Doyle, 1972). Since subscale scores are likely to be less reliable, decisions based on these scores require more caution in their application.

One study has examined the internal consistency of colleague ratings. Hildebrand, Wilson, and Dienst (1971) derived five scales of four to eight three-point items each and asked 119 faculty to rate 84 previously identified "best" instructors. Items that would have required the raters' attendance at lectures or seminars were excluded. The internal consistency correlations (Cronbach's Alpha) of these five scales ranged from .65 to .86, these somewhat lower values than were found for student ratings being partly a function of the restrictive three-point rating scale. No similar studies of self or administrator ratings have been found.

Stability, or retest reliability, is a measure of reliability based on rater agreement over time. In a retest study, a questionnaire is given twice to the same people, the administrations separated by some period of time (a few minutes, a few days, a few weeks, or longer). To the extent that the ratings are the same on both occasions, the data are said to be stable. The less random error there is in the ratings, the more the two administrations will be able to correlate with each other and the more reliable they will be. Stability and internal consistency are independent of one another. Heterogeneous item content as well as homogeneous can be stable or unstable.

But just as not all ratings need to be internally consistent, neither need they be stable. For example, if the instructor changes between initial and subsequent ratings, the ratings should reflect those changes. In the same vein, ratings of static traits like height should be more stable than ratings of dynamic states like mood, and ratings given closer together in time should usually be more stable than those given further apart.

While it would be important to know the extent to which ratings change over time as a function of random or systematic rater, task, and situational factors as distinguished from instructor and course factors, the typical retest study is only marginally adequate to the task, given that instructor changes are uncontrolled and trait differences usually unexamined. It would also be important to know in these studies if the instructor received a report of his ratings after the first evaluation, since the furnishing of such a report could

---

[b] Simply adding to the set more items that correlate with the initial items increases internal consistency.

create a dilemma for some intended uses of the data: no change could be interpreted as indicating high reliability but little usefulness for improving teaching, while change could be taken as indicating lower reliability but greater usefulness. Perhaps the best way to study stability would be to have raters rate a videotaped lecture on two or more occasions. No such study seems to have appeared in the literature. Those studies that have appeared, however, within these limitations, indicate a reasonable degree of stability for student ratings (Table 3–2).

No retest reliability study of self, administrator, or colleague ratings of college instruction seems yet to have been published, but Morsh and Wilder (1954, p. 16) cite several early studies of supervisor ratings of elementary and secondary school teachers. The stability coefficient reported in those studies range from .18 to .93, with most in the .50s or higher. The stability of these ratings approximates that reported in Table 3–2 for student ratings.

Although these studies seem to indicate that student ratings and perhaps colleague and supervisor ratings are or can be made to be reasonably free of random error, neither retest reliability nor homogeneity is sufficient indication of the absence of systematic error, error that is constant for a given person or a given group. In fact, both homogeneity and stability can be artificially inflated by systematic error. For example, if the raters are letting their specific ratings be influenced by their overall impression of the ratee (halo effect), then the resultant spurious intercorrelation among the rated traits will serve to increase the internal consistency of the item set. And if raters are tending to mark the midpoints of the rating scales (error of central tendency), this phenomenon, over repeated administrations, will artificially increase stability.

Other methods than internal consistency and stability have been devised to measure freedom from random error but which, at the same time, seem somewhat less vulnerable to artificial inflation. One such method assumes that instructors differ from one another in terms of the various specific aspects of teaching behavior. Accordingly, the mean ratings of a substantial number of instructors should at least not all be the same. If the mean ratings are all the same, then either the instructors are all the same—an unlikely event—or the ratings are biased. If the mean ratings are identical, the cause could be either random or systematic error or some combination of the two. If the ratings are not identical, they are likely to be relatively free of random error (especially since computing means neutralizes or cancels out much random error) and, to some extent at least, free from most kinds of systematic error. Whitely, Doyle, and Hopkinson (1973) employed this method as part of a larger study and found that mean ratings on many traits did differ across instructors in a multi-section course, but that (as would be expected) ratings of the course and its mechanics did not differ across sections.

Table 3–2

Illustrative Studies of the Stability of Student Ratings of Instructors

Study	Student Sample	Number and Kind of Items	Time Interval	Stability
Remmers and Brandenburg (1927)	30–33 in 3 courses	10 ten-point ratings (PRSI[a])	3 days	.42–.92
Root (1931)	200 in one course	50 item checklist	4 weeks	.95
Lovell and Haner (1955)	105 in 4 courses	36 force-choice tetrads	2 weeks	.89
Costin (1968)	Unreported number, mostly in sections of one large course	5 subscales, 3–5 five-point ratings each	Mid-semester to end of semester	.41–.87
Kooker (1968)	92 in 4 sections	7 subscales, 7–14 five-point ratings each	2 weeks	.58–.87
		Total scores		.91
Costin (1971)	Same 219 of 11 instructors	4 subscales, 4–7 five-point ratings each (factor scores)	2 weeks 2 weeks	.67–.77
Kohlan (1973)	271 in eight classes	3 subscales, 4–7 five-point ratings each	2nd day of semester	.55–.70
		Single general five-point ratings	2nd day of semester	.58

[a] Purdue *Rating Scale for Instructors*

This method too has its weaknesses, however: the unverifiable assumption that the sampled instructors do differ from one another and the inability to identify the sources of error in ratings that do not differ. The first problem has been largely resolved by the rather frequent research strategy of asking students to recall and rate good, average, and poor instructors. The means of these three groups are compared, and items which differentiate among the groups are considered reliable. That this is an important step in the construction of a questionnaire is supported by the fact that Doyle (1972), using the admittedly stringent criterion of highly significant differences among all possible pairs of means, found 348 of 588 items unreliable in this sense. For other applications of the same or similar procedures, see Meehl (1941), Wherry (1952), Gibb (1955), Lovell and Haner (1955), Morsh (1955), Patton and Meyer (1955), Cosgrove (1959), Remmers and Weisbrodt (1965), and Hildebrand, Wilson, and Dienst (1971). Of course, this method is only as dependable as the initial subjective partitioning of instructors into good, average, and poor categories. It is surprising, therefore, that no published study has apparently tried to make this categorization on the basis of student-outcome measures, especially those objectively appraised. Were this not the case, some of the brouhaha concerning ratings and student achievement might have been avoided (see chapter 4).

The problem of identifying the nature and extent of systematic errors is a complicated one. Rather than attempting to devise a general method applicable to all kinds of systematic error, many researchers have found it more efficient to try to identify different types of systematic error and to select methods adequate to assess the influence of each.

Leniency is one kind of systematic error. As already indicated, Sharon (1970; see also Sharon and Bartlett, 1969) pointed to the presence of considerable leniency error in some kinds of student ratings. When students were told that the ratings they were about to give might be used for personnel purposes, and when they expected to have to explain their ratings personally to the instructor, their ratings were markedly more generous than when given "for research purposes only." Earlier work by Lovell and Haner (1955) had found similar results. (In both these cases, forced-choice scales were considerably less biased than numerical scales, but see chapter 2 for an elaboration of the problems associated with forced-choice scaling.)

Centra (1973a) compared student ratings and self ratings for leniency error and found that, although there were exceptions, instructors as a group gave themselves more favorable ratings than did their students. He also found (1974) a very strong leniency effect in colleague ratings. On one fairly typical item, of 460 ratings on a five-point scale, 431 of them (93.7%) were either "excellent" or "good," and only one rating was "poor." Although he notes that the presence of a colleague in the classroom could have stimulated instructors to do their best during those sessions, Centra still considers leniency error to be more pronounced in self and colleague ratings than in student ratings.

Another kind of systematic error in ratings is halo effect, the tendency to let one's overall impression of the ratee influence ratings of specific traits. That halo error exists in student ratings has been suggested by correlation matrices which show high relationships among ratings of what one would expect to be quite distinct traits and outcomes (e.g., "organization" and "regard for students" in Doyle, 1972) and similarly by factor analyses that place disparate traits under the same dimension (e.g., "clarity of explanation" and "skill in observing student reactions" in Isaacson et al., 1964). Both of these studies indicate the presence of some degree of inter-trait association that is probably due to halo error. Another demonstration of halo effect is found in Holmes's (1972) observation that when he gave students lower grades than they had expected and deserved, the ratings from these students were lower on 10 of 19 items than from students who had received their expected and deserved grades. The lowering of ratings on a *variety* of items signifies the operation of halo effect. On the other hand, halo effect is not so powerful that stable factor structures cannot emerge (e.g., Isaacson et al., 1964; Gibb, 1955; Deshpande, Webb, and Marks, 1970; Bejar and Doyle, 1974c; Doyle and Whitely, 1974), and Remmers and Brandenburg (1927) noted only trivial intercorrelation among the rated traits.

Contrast error, identified by Murray (1938) and elaborated upon by Guilford (1954, pp. 280–81), could increase or decrease ratings on particular items depending on how the rater perceives himself and the ratee in terms of the traits represented by those items. Because the direction and distribution of the contrast effect would be extremely difficult to predict, this kind of error will be considered random rather than systematic, and the techniques described above will be assumed to include it in their measurement. No explicit study of contrast error appears in any of the faculty evaluation literature.

Guilford (1954, pp. 280–88) has proposed a statistical approach for the estimation and correction of leniency and halo errors, as well as contrast effect, in a given rating situation. His procedure identifies the sources and kinds of error algebraically and employs analyses of variance to determine the amount of each kind of error in the data and to adjust for it. (See also Wherry, 1952.) This methodology is for research use, however, not for routine application; it affects interrater and intertrait correlations but does not change the ratee's means. Nor does it consider errors of central tendency or the proximity and logical effects. Guilford's illustrative data are of as much interest as his method, for they consist of ratings of the creative performance of seven research scientists by three senior scientists. The data indicate the presence of a substantial amount of halo effect in these colleague or supervisor ratings, but inconsequential amounts of leniency and contrast error. Thus Guilford's and Centra's findings with regard to leniency effect are inconsistent, although the fact that Guilford's sample included only three raters and seven ratees speaks against the generalizability of his findings.

The effect of errors of central tendency is akin to that of halo error, namely a diminution of the distinctness of the scales, and much the same correlational data as suggest halo can be taken as an indication of central tendency.

Similar in certain ways to one another are the proximity and logical errors. Proximity error involves rating adjacent items similarly simply because they are adjacent, not because the ratee possesses a similar amount of both traits. Logical error entails rating items similarly because the traits they represent "ought" to be found together, not necessarily because they are found together in a particular ratee. Proximity error can be assessed by examining the average correlation of adjacent items in comparison to the average correlation of those same items when not adjacent. That proximity error exists in personnel ratings was demonstrated by Stockford and Bissell (1949). The effect of this error should be principally upon the structure (intercorrelation) of the ratings and depends upon the serial arrangement of the items. If the adjacent items are similar in content, proximity error should lead to more clearly interpretable dimensions from factor analysis; if the adjacent items are dissimilar, the structures are more likely to be composed of those dissimilar items and hence more difficult to interpret. In either case, the adjacent-item means may be unduly similar. Logical error could be measured by comparing the intercorrelation of rated traits to the intercorrelation of traits otherwise measured, which was the approach taken by Newcomb (1931) to demonstrate the existence of this type of error. As a result of logical error, the intercorrelation of logically related traits increases and the mean ratings on these traits may become excessively similar.

A more elaborate version of logical error is the relatively recent notion of "implicit theories" of behavior (see Schneider, 1973, for a general review). In the context of student ratings, implicit theories are preconceptions of how a particular instructor should behave, based on the rater's accumulated experience with instructors and instruction. Whitely and Doyle (1974a) asked one group of students to sort rating items into categories on the basis of similar content, this categorization being taken as an explication of implicit theories. Other groups of students were asked to rate their instructors with a questionnaire composed of those same items. Item-response ratings were factor analyzed and the resulting structure compared to that from a parallel analysis of the categorizations. The extreme similarity between the rating structure and the categorization structure led the authors to conclude that implicit theories were indeed operating in the ratings and constituted another potential source of bias with effects similar to those of logical error. A subsequent study by the same authors (1974*b*), however, compared the categorization structure to a structure resulting from a factor analysis of *mean* ratings.[c] The high degree of similarity between the two structures suggested that students' implicit theories of instructor behavior are to a large extent commensurate with the patterns of traits and behaviors that actually occur in instructors. Implicit theories, then, may exist, but they apparently do not exert much influence on student ratings.

If implicit theories are built upon the students' accumulation of experience, so too are expectations, although the latter may be modified on the basis, for example, of the reputation of a particular department, course, or instructor. Expectations are broader than, and include, implicit theories. Bejar and Doyle (1974*a*) examined the effects of expectations on student ratings. Choosing a course the instructors for which were not named in the class schedule, and before the instructor appeared for the first class session, the investigators asked students to rate what they expected their instructors to be like. At the end of the course, the students evaluated their instructors with slightly reworded items. Comparisons between the factor structures of the initial and subsequent ratings indicated that two distinct processes had been operating, namely expectation and evaluation. The categories or factor structures underlying both processes were the same, but the students' use of these categories differed. Furthermore, an attempt statistically to predict evaluation ratings from expectation ratings was unsuccessful. The authors concluded that less than 1% of the variability in evaluation was predictable from expectation, that is, that students reliably distinguish what they expect of an instructor from what they actually get.

In similar vein, Treffinger and Feldhusen (1970), during the first week of a course, asked students to rate their general impressions of courses and instructors at Purdue. During the last week of the term the students used the same scales to rate their actual course instructor. General impression did to an extent predict the evaluations of the particular instructors, but the prediction was quite weak, accounting for only about 10% of the variance. This slightly different finding from Bejar and Doyle's may be explained by the fact that Treffinger and Feldhusen's students had already seen their actual instructor when they gave their generalized ratings. The generalized ratings, then, may have been biased by the introduction of the

---

[c] Mean ratings, because their computation averages out student individual differences and a considerable portion of ratings error, are taken as descriptions of trait *occurrence* in instructors. Item response ratings are taken as descriptions of trait *usage* by raters.

actual instructor. A subsequent report by Bejar and Doyle (1974b) lends some credence to this explanation. Further research of this sort—for example, how early in a term do impressions become crystallized enough to predict evaluations?—seems warranted.

In the light of all these studies, what conclusions can be drawn about the reliability of student ratings via-à-vis other ratings and for the various purposes of evaluation?

First of all, even without particular efforts to increase or assure the homogeneity and stability of student ratings, these data seem reasonably free from random error, their internal consistency and retest coefficients tending usually to be in the .60s and above. Some systematic errors, notably halo and leniency, are present, but again the extent of these errors is not great. Recalling the standard proposed at the beginning of this chapter, it would seem that student ratings gathered by means of any but the most poorly constructed rating scales will be sufficiently reliable to be used for course improvement purposes.

Using student ratings as a basis for personnel decisions is another matter. The reliability of measures used for this purpose must be greater than that displayed by the typical "home-grown" rating scale. Both random error and systematic error need to be further reduced. The conclusion, however, is not to avoid using student ratings in personnel decisions but rather to take steps to improve the precision of these measures. One avenue to improved reliability is greater attention to the construction of rating scales. Chapter 2 detailed a number of techniques for reducing ambiguity and enhancing differentiation, and additional albeit sometimes more complicated techniques are available (see Guilford, 1954, especially chapter 11; Nunnally, 1967, especially chapters 2 and 7; Thorndike, in Jackson and Messick, 1967; and Doyle, 1972, especially chapter 2). The fact that a number of researchers have demonstrated that it is indeed possible to construct instruments that gather highly reliable student ratings indicates that local efforts to do the same would not be in vain.

Refined scales increase the *potential* for highly reliable data but do not assure that that potential will be achieved. In addition to good instruments is the need for motivated and capable raters. Student motivation can probably best be enhanced by demonstrations that these ratings are taken seriously, and also by assuring that the scales students are asked to use are unambiguous and germane. Rater competency can be increased by practice, by forewarning raters of what they will be asked to rate, and even by alerting them to the kinds of errors, both random and systematic, to which their ratings are subject.

Yet not even taking all these steps will assure that *every* set of ratings will be reliable enough for use in personnel decisions. Consequently, important decisions should never be made on the basis of a single set of ratings. Rather, such decisions should require the confluence of evaluations of various tasks and potentials at various times, and by different groups of people. More than one set of student ratings should be examined, and student ratings should be supplemented by other kinds of information.

Among these other kinds of information are colleague ratings, administrator or supervisor ratings, and self ratings. The literature appears to be deficient in studies of the reliability of these kinds of data. The very few directly relevant studies suggest that colleague, administrator, and self ratings gathered on well constructed ratings scales will probably not be much more influenced by random error than student ratings. They may, however, be more subject to systematic error, especially leniency effect. That this should be the case is not surprising. Not only might one quite realistically expect a greater degree of leniency from colleagues, administrators, and one's self than from students, but colleagues and administrators are often disadvantaged by being asked to rate what they have had at best relatively little opportunity to observe. And self ratings, though of distinct usefulness for instructional improvement, are too open to bias of all sorts to supplant other information for personnel decisions. Until empirical evidence argues otherwise, data of these sorts should only supplement student ratings. And, because much more is known about student ratings than about other kinds of ratings, in case of conflict between information from students about a person's instructional effectiveness and similar information from colleagues, administrators, or the instructor himself, the burden of proof lies with the latter.

As far as reliability is concerned then, the conclusion is that student ratings can routinely be used for purposes of instructional improvement, but that if they are to be used for personnel decisions steps will have to be taken to improve their reliability over that of ratings gathered by the typical instrument constructed without attention to data quality. Moreover, demonstrations of the reliability of a particular instrument in a particular setting perhaps ought to be required, and any set of data should be buttressed by additional and diverse sets. The reliability and safeguards to be required of data to be used for other purposes—e.g., advising students—will depend on local assessment of the harm that could accrue to individuals if those decisions were made on the basis of imprecise information.

Finally, it must be emphasized that reliability is a necessary but insufficient quality of data. The next chapter will consider the other requisite quality.

4 Validity

Validity means meaning. Validation is the process of attributing meaning to data. To grasp this notion of meaning attribution one might think of responses to a rating scale as nothing more than a set of meaningless numbers in wait for meaning to be given them by one operation or another. Since the more these numbers are studied the more meaning they take on, validation can be conceived of as an incremental process.

The procedures that give meaning to data can be classified on a continuum from subjective to objective. They are subjective to the extent that they rely on human judgment or reason; they are objective to the extent that they depend upon empirical fact and quantitative technique. The distinction is in terms of the preponderance of one or the other kind of operation, for all validation includes both fact and judgment.

Subjective Validation

The first step in the incremental validation process is to examine the wording of an evaluative statement: What do the words themselves say? If ratings say "The instructor raised challenging questions," are these words dependable? At this level if a statement is reliable, it is to that same extent valid. This equivalence of reliability and validity is perhaps most clearly seen in the case of a rating scale. If responses to that scale are demonstrated to be free of error (as described in the preceding chapter), then they mean what their words say. Less clear is the equivalence of reliability and validity in narrative evaluations, but the equivalence holds. If a narrative statement is clearly given and clearly understood, it too means what its words say. Indeed, some authors have argued that this level of validity is the only one that can be achieved by evaluative ratings, because there is no criterion beyond judgment to which to appeal (e.g., Kelly, in Meehl, 1941, p. 58; Remmers, 1927, 1928, 1928; Whitely, 1974).

But there often is information that supplements the wording of evaluations. The meaning of a statement can be expanded by knowledge about certain characteristics of the statement or of the question that elicited the statement. Wherry's extensive research on student ratings demonstrates this point.

Wherry (1952) developed a pool of some 900 different rating items gleaned from university student essays on effective and ineffective instruction. He had people rate each item for certain attributes and from those ratings he computed five statistical indices for each item.[a] He then intercorrelated and factor analysed the 300 "best" items and found twelve themes or factors that seemed to summarize them (see Table 4–1). Each of the five statistical indices, the correlation of the items with all other items, and the relationship of the items to each theme or factor all add meaning beyond that conveyed solely by the wording. Thus Wherry provided a pool of studied ratings stems about which, in addition to their wording, the following information is known: the extent to which the trait is found in ranked better and worse instructors, the willingness of student raters to rate instructors on the trait, the ease with which students judged they could estimate the presence of the trait in an instructor, and the relationship of that trait to other rated traits and to themes or factors of rated traits.

Wherry then studied each of these 300 items in terms of nine more attributes, including how certain the raters felt concerning the meaning of the rating, how sharp or unambiguous they felt the meaning to be, and how confident they were in their ability to observe the trait in a given instructor. The meaning of these items is further extended by knowledge about each of these attributes and is thus considerably greater than that conveyed only by the wording of the items. (More recent items pools that include information about the extended meaning of ratings have been developed by Hildebrand, Wilson, and Dienst, 1971, and Doyle, 1972.)

When more than a single item is involved, as in a typical questionnaire or ratings instrument, the subjective validity of the *collection* of items or statements can be also examined. Additional meaning is attributed to the set of statements by answering the question, Are all of the important dimensions of teaching represented here? To the extent that the answer is affirmative, the meaning of the collection is enhanced; and to the extent that it is negative, the meaning is restricted by the qualification.

One way to evaluate the comprehensiveness of a collection of evaluative questions is to set them against some criterion. One appropriate criterion might be a logical analysis of the teaching process, such as the rudimentary input/process/outcome model presented in chapter 1. To meet this model's requirements, a collection of items would have to treat input variables (the various traits of the instructor, the course materials, and the physical and

---

[a] The statistics were a Preference Index, Index of Preference Variability, Discrimination Index, Difficulty Index, and Index of Difficulty Variability. These statistics enabled Wherry to select the 300 best items—e.g., most discriminating, most preferred—for factor analysis. The fact that 600 items were eliminated from the original underscores the need for technical consultation in the development of questionnaires and rating scales.

social environments), cognitive process variables (e.g., cognition, memory, convergent and divergent thinking, and evaluation), and outcome variables (describing both cognitive and affective outcomes). The potential meaning of a collection of items, then, is diminished by any lacunae suggested by this outline. Its actual meaning is enhanced by completeness in terms of this criterion.

A second content criterion might come from factor analytic research on ratings items. As already indicated, factor analysis is a mathematical procedure for finding the underlying dimensions or summarizing themes of a set of variables. A number of reports of factor analyses of student ratings have been published. Although it is incautious to try to convey the content of a factor solely by means of its name,[b] Table 4–1 lists the names of the factors derived in ten different studies. The most influential of these reports is that by Isaacson, McKeachie, Milholland, Lin, Hofeller, Baerwaldt, and Zinn (1964). Using an instrument composed largely of items drawn from questionnaires then in use at the Ohio State University, University of Minnesota, and University of Michigan, Isaacson et al. found that six dimensions of student ratings repeatedly appeared: General Teaching Skills (defined by items like "Put his material across in an interesting way," "Explained clearly," and "All-around teaching ability"); Workload or Overload ("Assigned very difficult reading," "Asked for more than students could get done"); Course Structure ("Followed an outline closely," "Had everything going according to schedule"); Feedback to Students ("Told students when they had done a particularly good job"); Group Interaction ("The students in the class were friendly," "Students frequently volunteered their own opinions"); and Student/Teacher Rapport ("Was friendly," "Listened attentively to what class members had to say").

Other factor analysts have used more restricted ratings instruments and have found somewhat more focused dimensions. For example, Doyle and Whitely (1974) limited their instruments to items descriptive of instructor traits and behaviors. Five factors emerged in this study (and were replicated in Whitely and Doyle, 1974a): Expositional Clarity ("Clearly presented the subject matter"), Attitudes toward Students ("Was approachable"), Motivation of Interest in the Subject Matter ("Made you want to take more courses in the area"), Stimulation of Ideas and Thinking ("Raised challenging questions"), and Generalization of Course Content ("When appropriate, related course material to other areas of knowledge").

While any well executed factor analysis of a varied pool of course and instructor descriptions might provide a suitable criterion against which to

---

[b] A factor name is only the researcher's effort to summarize the meaning of a statistically interrelated group of items. As such, factor names depend on matters like the researcher's perspicuity and verbal fluency.

Table 4–1
Summary of Descriptions of Factor Analytic Studies

Study	Scale	Number of Subjects[a]	Number of Items	Names of Factors
Wherry	*Descriptive Check List* Ohio State University	200	300	Mastery, Organization, and Presentation of Subject Matter; Skill in Contact and Discipline of Students; Reasonableness of Demands on Student Time and Effort; Efficiency and Logicality of Classroom Management Procedures; Skill in Motivating, Inspiring, and Creating Confidence in Students; Conscientiousness in Carrying out of Duties and Justification of Actions; Impression Made on Class by Appearance and Physiology; Permissive vs. Rigid Presentation; Student vs. Subject Centered Approach; Friendliness vs. Coldness; Calmness vs. Irritability; Desire to Dominate vs. Satisfaction with Status
Crannell (1953)	Miami University *Rating Sheet*, Ohio	300	21	Course Result, Personal Interaction, Instructor Effort
Bendig (1954)	Purdue *Rating Scale for Instructors*	11 classes	10	Instructional Competencies, Instructor Empathy
Coffman (1954)	Oklahoma A & M *Rating Scale*	2000	19	Empathy, Organization, "Punctual-Neat-Normal," Verbal Fluency
Gibb (1955)	*Teacher Behavior Description Questionnaire*	119	165	Friendly, Democratic Behavior; Communication; Organization; Academic Emphasis

Table 4–1 continued

Study	Scale	Number of Subjects [a]	Number of Items	Names of Factors
Cosgrove (1959)	10 tetrads	100	150	Knowledge and Organization, Relations With Students, Plans and Procedures, Enthusiasm
Isaacson et al. (1964)	5-point scales, University of Michigan	297 male 392 female	46	Skill, Overload, Structure, Feedback, Group Interaction, Student-Teacher Rapport
Deshpende, Webb, and Marks (1970)	*Teacher Description Instrument*, Georgia Institute of Technology	32 classes	147	Motivation, Rapport, Structure, Clarity, Content Mastery, Overload, Evaluation Function, Use of Teaching Aids, Instructional Skills, Teaching Styles, Encouragement, Individual Assistance, Interaction, Text Adherence
Hildebrand, Wilson, and Dienst (1971)	4-point scales, University of California (Berkeley)	1015	91	Analytic/Synthetic Approach, Organization/Clarity, Instructor-Group Interaction; Instructor-Individual Student Interaction, Dynamism/Enthusiasm
Doyle and Whitely (1974)	*Student Opinion Survey*, University of Minnesota	174	49	Expositional Skills, Attitudes toward Students, Motivation of Interest in Subject, Stimulation of Ideas and Thinking, Generalization of Course Content

[a]Most studies used raw item responses, some used class means. For a discussion of the differences, if any, see Doyle and Whitely (1974), Bejar and Doyle (1974), and Linn, Centra, and Tucker (1974).

assess the completeness of a set of rating items, a more refined inspection should include some indication of the relative *importance* of each item or cluster of items. Indications of item importance might come from one's own personal estimate of which aspects of teaching are the most important for one's circumstances, from studies that have investigated faculty and/or student judgments of the importance of different ratings items (e.g., Wherry, 1952; Asher, 1969; Hildebrand, Wilson, and Dienst, 1971; and Doyle, 1972), or, for that matter, from any of the studies referred to here under the headings of subjective or objective validation.

Factor analysis can supply still other kinds of meaning. The fact that items in a factor are relatively highly intercorrelated suggests that knowing an instructor's rating on one item can imply something about his rating on other items in that factor. In the factor "Expositional Clarity," knowing an instructor's rating, say, on "Clearly presented the subject matter" allows some prediction of what his rating would be on "Uses good examples and illustrations." Thus some meaning about an item can be drawn from those items with which it correlates. Similarly, the relationship of global evaluative ratings like "over-all teaching ability" to specific rated traits and behaviors can help to explain the meaning of the global item. As just noted, Isaacson et al. (1964) found a general teaching skills factor that included (among others) the following items: "All-around teaching ability," "Class time was well spent," "He tried to increase the interest of the class members in his subject," "He made it clear how each topic fit into the course," and "He anticipated student difficulties before they arose." The meaning of the general summary item—"All-around teaching ability"—is enhanced by its relationship to the more specific items. Another example of this same point is found in Doyle and Whitely (1974), in which global items were analyzed for their relationships with separately derived specific-item factors. Table 4–2 shows the meaning of certain general rating items in terms of these specific factors. In this case, for example, over-all instructor effectiveness is defined in terms of the instructor's expositional skills, effectiveness at motivating student interest in the subject matter, and stimulation of ideas and thinking. Over-all instructor effectiveness is not so much influenced here by his attitudes toward students or generalization of course content.

Each of these operations has added a different kind of meaning to the items involved. Other operations are no doubt available. In fact, under the conceptualization of subjective validation adopted here, virtually any logical or judgmental procedure can be taken as assigning some kind of meaning to the data of evaluation. What those operations are and the meaning they supply depends on the particular items used, on the people whose judgment

Table 4–2

Relationships between General Rating Items and Specific-Item Factors

	Specific-Item Factors				
	I Attitudes toward Students	II Expo- sitional Skills	III Moti- vation of Interest	IV Stimu- lation of Thinking	V Generali- zation of Content
Liking for person	.55	.19	.16	−.09	.07
General teaching ability	.25	.50	.34	.16	.14
Attitudes about Teaching	.27	.47	.44	.26	.06
How much learned	−.02	.28	.35	.23	.16
How motivating	.19	.23	.44	.32	.30
Over-all teacher effectiveness	.14	.39	.39	.25	.15
Over-all course effectiveness	−.13	.07	.41	−.08	.02

Source: Doyle, K. O., Jr., and Whitely, S. E. 1974. Student ratings as criteria for effective teaching. *American Educational Research Journal, 11 (3),* 259–74. © 1974, American Educational Research Association, Washington, D.C. Reprinted by permission.

is involved, and on the specific circumstances surrounding the instruction and evaluation (goals, course format, etc.).

Objective Validation

The meaning of evaluation items is further extended by their relationship with more objective measures. This "criterion validation," in which the objective measures constitute criteria for additional meaning or criteria for the inferences to be made from the evaluations, can be direct or indirect. Direct criterion validation would involve setting a rating of a given trait against a separate, objective measure of that trait. Thus ratings of the trait "verbal fluency" could be objectively validated against the number of "um's" recorded in a given period of time. Or the trait "stimulates student interest" could be measured against pupillary dilation or galvanic skin response. Among the very few examples of direct validation of student ratings are two correlations in an extensive study by Elliott (1950). Elliott correlated student ratings of chemistry recitation and laboratory instructors' "knowledge of chemistry" with the instructors' scores on four achievement tests taken prior to the start of the semester (and one test taken after the completion of the semester). For the laboratory instructors, the correlation was a positive but nonsignificant .30; for the recitation instructors, the correlation was a positive significant .40. The students in these recitation sections, then, were significantly able to distinguish instructors who knew more about chemistry from those who knew less.[c]

And, across eighteen sections of introductory economics, McKeachie, Lin, and Mann (1971) found a significant positive correlation (.44), between ratings of the instructor's effectiveness in changing students' beliefs and changes in the students' scores on a test that involved distinguishing between naive and sophisticated beliefs about the substance of economics.

Indirect criterion validation [d] involves ramifications of the evaluation items, usually ramifications having to do with some kind of change in the students. Apparent change in student interest as a result of experience with a particular instructor was the criterion in at least two studies. McKeachie and Solomon (1958) studied high-enrollment undergraduate psychology courses over a three-year period. These eight courses were ranked in three ways: first, according to the percentage of students actually enrolling in more advanced psychology courses; second, on the basis of student responses to a single evaluation item about the course instructor's general teaching effectiveness; and third, with respect to a single rating item about the effectiveness of the course itself. In two of the five semesters studied, evaluative rankings were significantly correlated with the percentages of students enrolling in further courses. Wherry (1952) found low-to-moderate relationships between adjectival and checklist evaluations and students' stated intent to continue in the field (perhaps more of a subjective criterion) and no relationship between forced-choice evaluations and the same criterion. One should be cautious about drawing conclusions from either of these studies. The inconsistency of results across Wherry's formats suggests the presence of some kind of "method error" in the ratings,[e]

---

[c] It is interesting to note that in another part of the same study Elliott found that the correlations between tested instructor knowledge of chemistry and tested student achievement (adjusted for initial ability) ranged from $-.01$ through $-.56$. That is, he found a tendency for students to learn less in freshman chemistry from recitation and laboratory instructors who knew more about chemistry, especially about freshman chemistry. While this result may be explainable in terms of differential teaching motivation on the part of the instructors, it remains a phenomenon that deserves further study.

[d] Indirect validation can conceptually involve an "ultimate" criterion or an "intermediate" criterion. An example of an ultimate criterion, after Thorndike, is: "Earning a decent livelihood in a satisfying and mentally healthy competition and cooperation with others." Since ultimate criteria are rarely if ever measureable, criteria are substituted which seem reasonably related to ultimate criteria, namely intermediate criteria such as learning.

[e] "Method error," or findings dependent more on methodology than substance, was the point of Wherry's comparison of ratings formats. His argument was that "intent to continue" is a biased, amorphous criterion and that sharp, unbiased ratings—i.e., forced-choice ratings—should *not* correlate with it.

and the failure of McKeachie and Solomon's results to replicate across all terms indicates that the results are not dependable. Furthermore, as Wherry himself points out about the "intent-to-continue" criterion:

. . . we have no way of knowing whether or not its presence in a given student was caused by the instructor or by factors independent of the instructor. . . . A change in this criterion might be attributable to the instructor, but we have no data on intention prior to taking the present course.

Thus no firm conclusion can yet be drawn about the meaning of student evaluations in terms of change of student interest expressed either by stated intention to continue in a field of study or by actual continuation.

Other kinds of meaning could be assigned to student evaluations by relating them to measures of student learning. Student learning can be cognitive, in which case it can be recall of material, understanding of material, integration of material into a broader framework, ability to evaluate the goodness of material, and so forth. Student learning can also be affective, like development of appreciation for the material or modification of student values or even their personal philosophies. In spite of the breadth and depth of possible measures of student learning, most objective validation studies have been concerned exclusively with those kinds of learning that are more or less conveniently measured by classroom examinations. Since the content of these is rarely reported, it is quite probable that affective achievement is not involved in these studies and that even within cognitive achievement, most measures have more to do with recall of facts and basic grasp of material than with higher forms of learning. Most learning-criterion measures, then, are probably less meaningful themselves than one might like them to be.

Perhaps the earliest study of learning and student evaluations was conducted by Root (1931). Root had an instructor combine a student ratings scale, administered bimonthly, with critical essays by students and a more detailed questionnaire designed to probe the reasons for any adverse ratings. In the same course the following year, the same instructor reportedly tried to change his behavior as suggested by the previous year's evaluation. Initial ratings in the second year showed "substantial" improvement over those from the first year. Root equated both classes for intelligence, college aptitude, and previous knowledge of the subject matter. On the course examination, the mean of the second year's class exceeded that of the first year's by almost 20 points (68.6 vs. 86.5), a difference both practically and statistically significant.

This early report does not provide enough information for a thorough critique, but while the situation described is perhaps a bit unrealistic in the amount of evaluation undertaken, the study does provide at least some indication of a positive relationship between ratings and learning as measured by a course examination.

A more typical research design for studying the ratings/learning issue involves a multi-section course with a common final examination. Mean student ratings from each section are correlated with mean course-examination scores that have somehow been adjusted to compensate for differing levels of initial student ability across sections. These "residualized achievement scores" are taken as measures of student learning.

A study using this design was reported by Remmers, Martin, and Elliott (1949). Students in thirty-seven laboratory and recitation sections of beginning chemistry rated their instructors on the *Purdue Rating Scale for Laboratory and Recitation Instructors in General Chemistry*. The ratings form had two twelve-item parts, the first set of ratings for laboratory instructors, the second set for recitation instructors. (The items from this instrument are included in Table 4–3.) Mean chemistry grades for the sections were statistically predicted from mean orientation-test scores, and the differences between actual and predicted grades was computed. Instructors whose students achieved higher than predicted were considered the "better" teachers; those whose students underachieved, the "poorer" ones. If the ratings reflected this more objective separation, they would be considered validated in terms of student learning. Table 4–3 shows that all twelve differences are in the positive direction, that is, the objectively better instructors were rated more highly. But only three of the items showed differences large enough to be statistically significant. For the recitation instructors, the results were similar. Most ratings reflected the objective separation, but only two of them significantly so. (Two differences were in the negative direction, though trivial in magnitude.)

Remmers et al. concluded:

There is warrant for ascribing validity to student ratings not merely as measures of student attitude toward instructors (for which validity and reliability are synonymous) but also as measured by what students actually learned of the content of the course.

Elliott (1950) undertook a more detailed study of the same sort. Instructors in thirty-six laboratory and recitation sections of a freshman chemistry course were rated by their students on the rating instrument just described. The instructors in this study were inexperienced first-year graduate students, each responsible for two sections of the course. The instructors were very closely supervised by the professor in charge of the course; the subject matter covered each week was the same for each instructor, the process for handing back and discussing examinations was outlined in detail, etc. In short, the content and mechanisms of the course were highly regimented. Thus differences across sections would most likely rise from

Table 4–3

Comparison of Mean Ratings for Objectively Measured "Better" and "Worse" Instructors

	After Remmers, Martin, and Elliott, 1949				After Elliott, 1950
	Means				
	"Better" N = 17	"Worse" N = 13	Dif- ference	Prob- ability	Correlations N = 36
Laboratory					
1. Interest in chemistry	4.082	3.869	.213	.12	.195
2. Knowledge of chemistry	4.347	4.031	.316	.05	−.018
3. Effectiveness as a teacher	3.953	3.654	.299	.08	.233
4. Fairness	4.606	4.508	.098	.23	.234
5. Attitude	4.135	3.969	.166	.24	.367**
6. Conduct during labora- tory period	4.476	4.346	.130	.23	.431**
7. Grading of experiments and reports	4.365	4.131	.234	.09	.109
8. Returning dailies and tests	4.335	4.108	.227	.10	.303
9. Care of communal appa- ratus	4.382	4.215	.167	.09	.050
10. Supervision during tests and dailies	4.482	4.231	.251	.05	.262
11. Rating as compared to other instructors at Pur- due University	4.000	3.454	.546	.03	.318
12. Should instructors be kept if suitable replace- ments are available?	3.576	3.223	.353	.07	.335**
	N = 17	N = 12			
Recitation					
1. Interest in subject	4.106	4.025	.081	.30	.099
2. Knowledge of subject	4.318	4.133	.185	.17	−.079
3. Effectiveness as a teacher	4.024	3.883	.141	.20	.255
4. Fairness	4.594	4.617	−.023	.40	.318
5. Attitude	4.153	4.283	−.130	.25	.310
6. Clarity of presentation	3.806	3.492	.314	.08	.176
7. Voice and mannerisms	4.282	4.033	.249	.13	.208
8. Coverage of assigned work	4.094	3.708	.386	.02	.242
9. Method of instruction	3.929	3.892	.037	.40	.272
10. Educational effectiveness of recitation	3.794	3.750	.044	.38	.357**
11. Rating as compared to other instructors at Pur- due University	3.935	3.642	.293	.05	.344**
12. Should instructors be kept if suitable replace- ments are available?	3.582	3.400	.182	.19	.171

** Significant at $p < .01$.

Source: Adapted from Remmers, Martin, and Elliott (1949) and Elliott (1950). © 1949, 1950 Purdue University. Reprinted by permission of Measurement and Research Center, Purdue University.

differences among the instructors. The mean section ratings, for laboratories and recitation sections separately, were correlated with the mean differences between students' actual and predicted grades. These correlations are also shown in Table 4–3.

None of these correlations is especially impressive in its magnitude, including the statistically significant ones, but there again appears to be at least some meaning in terms of this learning criterion that can be attached to some of these ratings.

A recent and highly controversial study of instruction of this sort—i.e., recitation and/or laboratory instruction—was conducted by Rodin and Rodin (1972). Because of the considerable national attention this study received, and because of the force and import of its conclusion, it will receive somewhat extended discussion here.

Rodin and Rodin studied an undergraduate calculus class in which a single lecturer taught the combined class three days a week and graduate students met with smaller groups of students twice a week to answer questions about lectures and homework and to administer test problems or go over preceding ones. The study focused on the recitation sections. At the end of the term, students in the twelve sections were asked to rate the graduate assistants on an item that read:

What grade would you assign to his total teaching performance? (A, B, etc.)

(Ratings on a number of other apparently more specific items were collected, but no information about these data was presented in the report.) The course examination consisted of forty "paradigm problems"—any error, no matter how trivial, caused the whole problem to be marked wrong, but students could retake variants of any problem as many as six times. The score was the number of problems (and variants) correct. This score was adjusted for varying student ability by statistically removing initial ability in calculus as indexed by performance in the preceding quarter of this three-quarter course.

The correlation between these adjusted examination means and the mean student ratings was −.75. From this correlation, the Rodins argued that "students rate most highly instructors from whom they learn least" (see also M. Rodin, 1973).

These data would add a very special meaning to student evaluations—namely that they should be used in precisely the opposite fashion than usually intended, that is, they should be used as *negative* indexes of instructional effectiveness in recitation sections—were it not for some quite severe substantive and technical deficiencies in the research. Substantively, the study appears to be not so much an examination of the relationship between student evaluations and teaching/learning, as between student evaluations and the ancillary activities of question-answering, test-giving, and problem-working. From this perspective, one might even *expect* a negative relationship with a learning measure in this case, since better students should have less need or use for these supplementary offerings and would therefore be expected to give less favorable evaluations.

Even if this study had involved what is more commonly meant by teaching, its methodology operates against drawing any conclusions from it. The striking datum is the very high *negative* correlation: $-.75$. However, as in many if not most studies of objective validation, there is a very wide confidence interval or region of uncertainty surrounding this statistic. Because of the relatively small number of sections upon which the correlation was based, the correlation is quite unstable and could easily be, say, from .60 to .74 *more or less than* the reported value (i.e., $-.75 \pm .60$). The correlation is indeed statistically significant, but not so striking as it might appear to the casual reader.

Other problems lead one to doubt the acceptability of this significant negative correlation. First, the dependability of the correlation depends on the criterion measure as well as on the ratings, and the criterion measure is quite difficult to assess. Although the tests themselves seems quite carefully devised, the test scores are not the data that were analyzed. Rather, class grades were substituted for the more direct criterion of percent of paradigms passed. This substitution loses information and contributes further to the instability of the correlation. Furthermore, the scatterplot indicates a distinct lack of variability in the average grade the classes received. Scores ranged from just greater than 3.0 to just over 3.5, and most of the variation is due to a single score in the plot. Such constricted variance suggests that the differences among sections in "learning" may be totally accounted for by error. This is particularly the case because of the use of grades as criteria; it is entirely possible that a class that passed more paradigms than another could have received a lower grade because of score proximity to the grade-cut points. Yet another problem concerns the reliability of the particular rating item employed. The variation of mean ratings across classes may have been entirely within the range specified by within-class consistency. Unfortunately, no information describing within-class consistency was reported. The most obvious measure would have been the standard deviation, and standard deviations—especially on global items —not infrequently approach 1.5 on five-point scales, a range that would quite easily encompass the variation in the means presented in this study.[f] To put the matter bluntly, the attention received by the Rodin and Rodin study seems disproportionate to its rigor, and their data provide little if any guidance in the validation of student ratings.

---

[f] More detailed critiques of this study appear in Doyle and Whitely, 1972, and in Frey, 1973.

While Remmers et al., Elliott, and Rodin and Rodin were concerned with what might be called ancillary instructional activities, a number of studies of what is perhaps closer to the common definition of teaching have also been published.

Wherry (1952) studied student evaluations and learning in twenty-one sections of introductory psychology taught by eleven advanced graduate students at the Ohio State University. The instructors used a common course outline and a common final examination but apparently had considerable latitude with regard to daily in-class activities. The examination was multiple-choice and drawn from a pool of preresearched test items. Examination scores were corrected for initial ability by partialling out ability scores. Rating scales in three different formats were randomly distributed to the students—adjectival ratings, checklists, and forced-choice scales, all of the same content. A total evaluation score was calculated by summing across all items in each kind of ratings instrument. The correlations between evaluations and the adjusted examination scores were:

Adjectival ratings	.04
Checklist	.01
Forced-choice scale	.42

When the forced-choice ratings are rescored to include only those whose discrimination and preference indices had replicated on an extra prestudy sample, the correlation rose to .51. The correlations are statistically significant, but again the confidence interval is rather large. The study does indicate a positive correlation between forced-choice ratings in general and this learning criterion, but because the ratings were summed across many different items, no conclusions can be drawn about the meaning of the individual items.

In a reply to the Rodin and Rodin paper, Frey (1973) studied evaluations of regular faculty teaching separate sections of two calculus courses. In the introductory course, eight regular faculty met with their classes of thirty to forty students for three lectures a week. The more advanced course (multidimensional calculus) was of similar format but consisted of five sections each taught by a different faculty member. (The students also met once a week for a given session with a teaching assistant, but the regular faculty were the focus of the study.) The faculty of each course devised a common syllabus and agreed on a common final examination. Scholastic Aptitude Test scores were used to adjust the students' examination scores. The ratings form consisted of eighteen seven-point ratings that were factor analysed into six dimensions. The correlations between mean ratings and adjusted examination scores for each of the six factors, for introductory and multidimensional calculus respectively, were: workload, .38, .51; student accomplishment, .84, .90; organization/planning, .87, .36; grading procedures, .65, .73; teacher's presentation, .91, .60; and teachers accessibility, .14, .49. All of these correlations are positive, and a number are significant. For both courses, student-rated student accomplishment was significantly correlated with the learning measure. In addition, ratings of organization/planning and teacher presentation in the introductory course were significantly associated with learning. The error band surrounding these statistics is even wider than in the Rodin and Rodin paper (because of the very small numbers of instructors) but with this caution the research is acceptable and provides an important item of information, namely that some ratings, but not others, tend to reflect student learning.

Doyle and Whitely (1974) studied twelve sections of a course in beginning French. An advanced graduate student was in charge of each section. Although two hours of lecture and drill were presented each week over closed-circuit television, the twelve instructors were responsible for selecting their own class materials and for teaching three hours a week. Textbook, syllabus, and examination were the same for all sections. The final examination, entirely in French, consisted of dictation, verb forms, sentence forms, plurals, and textual comprehension. Scores were the simple sum of correct responses, with 200 points possible. Minnesota Scholastic Aptitude Test scores were used to adjust the examinations for initial student ability. In addition, a subjective learning item was included: "How much would you say you learned from this instructor?" The ratings form, the *Student Opinion Survey,* consisted of six general and forty-nine specific items. Table 4–4 summarizes correlations between evaluations and the learning criteria. Evaluations on all six of the general items were significantly related to the subjective learning measure when raw item responses were used in the calculations; when mean section ratings were used, the correlations vanished, which suggests either the presence of methods error or that reliable differences among students were cancelled out by computation of the means.

Ratings of the instructor's "general teaching ability" and "over-all effectiveness" were significantly related to the objective learning measure on both data bases, although the confidence band surrounding the between sections correlation is quite wide.

The relationship between the specific-item factors and both criteria suggest a typically slight relationship between learning and ratings on instructor's "expositional skills" and "effectiveness at motivating student interest," as well as a hint of a relationship between the subjective measure of learning and "stimulation of ideas and thinking." It should be noted that there is no relationship in these data between an instructor's rated "attitudes toward students" and either learning measure. These findings seem reasonably consistent with Frey's.

Finally, McKeachie, Lin, and Mann (1971) reported a series of five studies that introduced some new dimensions to the validation of student

Table 4–4

Correlations between Ratings and Certain Learning Criteria

General Rating Items

Across Sections

	Liking for Person	General Teaching Ability	Attitudes about Teaching	How Much Learned	How Motivating	Overall Teacher Effect	Overall Course Effect
Final Examination	.01	.07	.04	.28 ***	.18 **	.26 ***	.20 **
How much learned?	.42 ***	.39 ***	.34 ***		.54 ***	.52 ***	.41 ***
Residualized Achievement	−.04	.18 **	.18 **	.25 ***	.18 **	.19 **	.24 ***

$**\ p \leq .01\ (r \geq .18)$
$***\ p \leq .001\ (r \geq .23)$

Between Sections

	Liking for Person	General Teaching Ability	Attitudes about Teaching	How Much Learned	How Motivating	Overall Teacher Effect	Overall Course Effect
Final Examination	.16	.35	.19			.13	
How much learned?							
Residualized Achievement	−.08	.51 *	.39 †			.49 *	

$†\ p \leq .10\ (r \geq .39)$
$*\ p \leq .05\ (r \geq .49)$
Blank cells indicate no correlation.

Specific-Item Factors

	I Attitudes toward Students	II Expo- sitional Skills	III Motivation of Interest	IV Stimulation of Thinking	V Generalization of Content
Final Examination	−.02	.34	.18	.00	−.01
How much learned?	−.02	.28	.35	.23	.16
Residualized Achievement	−.07	.31	.36	−.09	−.10

Source: Adapted from Doyle and Whitely, 1974. © 1974, American Educational Research Association. Reprinted by permission.

ratings. Two of these studies used the forty-six-item rating instrument described above, factored into six dimensions: skill, overload (difficulty), structure, feedback, interaction, and rapport (warmth). Means scores on the Introductory Psychology Criteria Test (Milholland, in McKeachie, Isaacson, and Milholland, 1964), adjusted for student ability, constituted the learning measures. This test was designed to measure some of the higher levels of cognitive achievement described in Bloom (1956). Across thirty-seven classes in general psychology, significant positive correlations were obtained for Skill, Feedback, Interaction, and Rapport, correlations of .28, .35, .30, and .42 respectively. The remaining correlations were essentially zero. So there is some basis for interpreting these kinds of ratings as reflections of *higher-order* student learning.

The authors reanalyzed the same data, but used a second criterion measure—mean scores on a more typical multiple-choice course examination [g]—*and* analyzed the data separately by sex of student. The results here were rather different from those of the first analysis. With the following exceptions, all of the correlations were nonsignificant: men's ratings of course difficulty were positively related to the course-examination criterion (.39); men's ratings of interaction among students were positively related to the higher-order cognition criterion (.33); and women's ratings of feedback to students were positively associated with both criteria (.33, .40). Women's ratings of instructor warmth tended to relate to learning of both kinds, but not significantly so. And women's ratings of structure tended to parallel their performance on the cognitive criterion, while men's ratings tended toward a negative association with that criterion measure.

In a replication involving sixteen general psychology instructors, two classes each, both men's and women's ratings of course difficulty correlated positively with the course examination criteria, and women's ratings of warmth correlated positively with the thinking measure. None of the other previous findings replicated, and there was a tendency for women's ratings of skill and interaction to relate negatively to cognitive achievement.

The remaining studies in this series found women's ratings of instructor skill correlated with performance on an essay test in general psychology, and with course examination scores and gains in "attitude sophistication" in a general economics course. As indicated earlier, women's ratings of the instructor's impact on beliefs were significantly related to their gains in attitude sophistication. None of the other correlations (sixty-four in all) in these studies were significant, partly due to the small number of sections available, and there are suggestions of negative correlations in a few cases (i.e., structure ratings and essay achievement for men in psychology, and

---

[g] It is not clear from the report whether scores on the criterion were adjusted for student ability, though the context implies that these corrections were performed.

structure ratings and course examination achievement for men in economics).

This series of studies was reported quite informally and the results are therefore difficult to evaluate. The authors conclude that skill ratings tend to reflect learning for women, that structure ratings tend to correlate positively with learning for women but perhaps negatively with learning for men, and that rapport ratings reflect learning on measures of higher order learning. Whether or not the data firmly support these conclusions is difficult to determine, but the important point raised by this series of studies is that failure to distinguish among rating items, among raters, and among criteria measures can conceal meaningful patterns of results.

What can one conclude from these studies? In order to reach any conclusion at all, it is necessary to distinguish between general ratings of, say, "over-all teaching ability" and specific ratings of particular instructor characteristics. There is no acceptable basis in these studies for accepting the hypothesis of a negative relationship between ratings of over-all instructor ability or effectiveness and learning-oriented criterion measures. On the other hand, neither are the data persuasive that there is a very large positive relationship. There does, however, appear to be a fairly consistent low-to-moderate positive correlation between general ratings and student learning.

The situation is more complex with regard to specific ratings. The nature of any relationship, and the appraisal of whether that relationship is appropriate or not, depends on the items involved. When the ratings are reliable, i.e., good descriptions of course and instructor characteristics, then the question is not whether the *ratings* are valid as indexes of student learning, but whether *the instructor and course characteristics described by those ratings* are related to student learning.

The problem is the old one: what constitutes effective teaching? From these learning-oriented studies of specific ratings, some extremely tentative conclusions can be drawn. There appears to be a tendency for the instructor's expositional clarity or presentation to relate to student learning as measured by fairly traditional course examinations (see the Frey and Doyle-Whitely results). There is no evidence of a relationship between learning of that sort and the instructor's attitudes toward students (sincerity, genuineness, respect, etc.), although rapport seems to contribute to higher-order learning at least for women. There is also some evidence (in McKeachie, Lin, and Mann) that some aspects of presentation, i.e., how structured it is, may be differentially effective. Women may learn some things better from more structured presentations, men from less structured ones.

What do all of these validity studies, subjective as well as objective, say about the meaning of student evaluations as they relate to improving teaching, personnel decisions, and advising students? A considerable quantity and variety of meaning is present in any reliable set of student evaluations. The most evident kind of meaning comes from the wording of the items and responses. In addition to this evident meaning is whatever can be inferred about a particular item or collection of items: meaning from item-selection procedures, from interitem correlations, from estimates of the importance of an item and the comprehensiveness of a collection, and, to some extent at least, meaning inferred from student outcomes.

No firm conclusion about the meaningfulness of student evaluations in general can be offered, since different instruments contain different items. Moreover, whether the meaningfulness of a particular set of data is sufficient and appropriate for the intended purpose depends on the instructional context as well as on one's own criteria for demonstrating validity. However, some general comments about meaningfulness in relation to purpose can be made. Evaluations for improving teaching require specific, diagnostically potent information that emphasizes the important aspects of instruction. Unfortunately, no compelling objective information yet exists to indicate what these important aspects might be, especially when one considers the interaction of specific course and instructor attributes with the particular instructional needs of different students pursuing diverse goals. In the absence of amply demonstrated empirical fact, it appears that an institution, a part of an institution, or—perhaps most appropriately—an instructor and his students are as good judges as anyone of what constitutes good teaching in particular situations. These judges can and should take advantage of the evident and inferential knowledge about student evaluations, including the few threads of knowledge concerning student outcomes in relation to specific instructor traits, but reasoned interpretation of all available specific information remains the most dependable route to meaningfulness of this sort.

Quite surprisingly, the situation seems somewhat *less* complex when it comes to student evaluations intended for use in personnel decisions. The difference is the fact that personnel decisions are more aided by general, summary evaluative statements than by specific course and instructor trait ratings. These statements of over-all teaching ability or effectiveness seem to have, in addition to their denotative meaning, meaning that is both subjectively and objectively inferrable. Subjectively, these general statements are defined by patterns of relationships with specific instructor and course characteristics that in general seem sensible, although the contextual interpretation suggested above is still called for. More objectively, these summary statements do appear to relate quite consistently, though not overwhelmingly, to student achievement measures. It appears that although different students might profit from different instructor and course attributes and although conceptualizations of effective teaching may vary from student to student, summary evaluations remain a function of the students' satisfaction with and achievement in the course.

Evaluations for use in student advising are similar to evaluations for each of the other general purposes. If one chooses to use specific trait ratings in advising, one faces the problem of differential treatment/need interactions. If one chooses summary evaluative statements, one can capitalize on the relative strengths of general items.

Whether the meaningfulness of student evaluations has been sufficiently documented in the literature is an open question. Most of the documentation comes from subjective validational procedures, and there is a general scepticism about subjective validation that seems steadfast even in light of gross and perhaps unavoidable deficiencies in most objective validation studies. This scepticism seems too strong; it has the unfortunate effect of overshadowing much legitimate knowledge that rests on human judgment. This is not to say that capricious subjectivity is the decision-maker's recourse, but rather that conscientious judgment, guided by empirical fact, is the most dependable foundation for meaning.

To determine the role of student evaluations in the various kinds of educational decisions requires a comparison among available kinds of information. Colleague, self, and administrator ratings share the validational difficulties of student ratings. Regardless of the source of specific ratings, identification of the traits to be rated will remain a problem. Whether colleague, self, or administrator general ratings are more or less meaningful than students' general ratings has yet to be demonstrated. No study as of yet seems to have compared colleague, self, or administrator evaluations to any kind of student outcome measure.

This tenuous state of affairs regarding the meaning of instructional evaluations from whatever source might be strengthened somewhat by a redirection of research efforts. For example, it is somewhat surprising that studies have not paid more explicit attention to other components of instruction than the teacher. One might expect course materials—textbooks and examinations, for example—to contribute significantly to learning. Ratings of the characteristics of these materials may help to identify the salient aspects of instruction.[h]

It is also surprising that more attention has not been directed to student motivation. McKeachie, Lin, and Mann convincingly demonstrated that neglect of individual differences among students can conceal a great deal of information. But one might wonder if categorizing students on the basis of variables like grade point, year in school, and even sex would be as fruitful as constructing typologies of students in motivational terms. Such typologies, especially as they interact with different instructional treatments, may contribute markedly to a definition of effective instruction.

---

[h] As noted in chapter 1, however, evaluations of course materials, because these materials are often only partially the instructor's responsibility, should be used only with considerable caution in administrative evaluations.

Correction of some common methodological deficiencies may lead to more interpretable data. Perhaps the single most difficult part of doing validational research is to locate a course that meets the requirements of good research design. Courses divided into many sections (preferably thirty or more) but with common content and common examinations, and especially those taught by senior faculty and geared toward multiple levels of learning, are very difficult to find. But, from a researcher's point of view at least, these courses are precious and should be sought out. Lacking such courses (and even with them) replications are important, especially replications involving the same people on different occasions. More attention, too, should be given to the basic goodness of measuring instruments. Investigations of the relationship between learning and ratings should only be done after the ratings have been shown to be reliable, because the meaningfulness of data is limited by their precision. Even more neglected have been the criterion measures. The reliability and validity of the course examinations or other achievement tests has rarely been evidenced. And the same problem holds for the tests used to adjust for differential student ability. Intelligence test scores, scholastic aptitude tests, and other general ability measures are not entirely persuasive bases against which to assess student progress. Subject-matter tests—reliable, valid, and parallel to the criterion measure—would seem to be more meaningful correction measures. And even the often used correlation coefficient is questionable. There seems to be little reason to expect a *linear* relationship between specific ratings and any kind of learning. Rather than predict that the more organized a lecturer is the more his students will learn, might not one expect that both too little organization *and too much* are inhibiting? Or at least that there is a threshold of organization below which communication is inhibited, but above which greater or less degrees of organization are largely irrelevant? Curvilinear statistics and threshold measures should be more often included in studies of student ratings.

Finally, it would appear that a major deficiency in research on the meaningfulness of evaluations is the lack of any reasonable theory of instruction to help guide the choice and assessment of ratings items. It is beyond the scope of this book—and, more to the point, beyond the capacity of this author—to furnish a detailed and coherent theory of instruction. However, a simple model may tempt others to refine it. The idea of person-environment correspondence dates at least to ancient Greece and has more or less recently appeared in works by Murray (1938), Pace (1963), Stern (1963), Astin and Holland (1961), Betz, Klingensmith, and Menne (1970), and—most influentially with regard to the present version—Dawis, Lofquist, and Weiss (1968). In brief, this model defines the learner in terms of abilities and needs, the environment in terms of ability requirements and need satisfiers. The relationship between the learner and

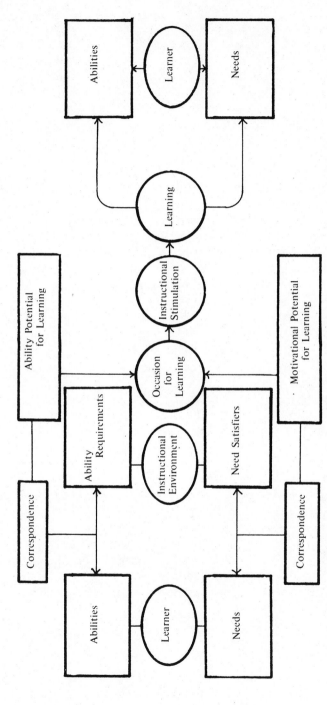

Source: Adapted from Dawis, Lofquist, and Weiss (1968). © 1968 Work Adjustment Project, Industrial Relations Center, University of Minnesota. Reprinted by permission.

Figure 4–1. Schematization of a Needs/Satisfiers Model of Learning.

the instruction he experiences is crucial. If the course's rewards, or need satisfiers, relate properly to the student's needs, the motivational potential for learning is created. If the student's abilities relate properly to the course's demands, or ability requirements, the ability potential for learning is established. If both the ability potential and the motivational potential exist in a given student in a given course, then the occasion for learning exists and exposure to the stimuli of the course (e.g., its content) leads to learning which in turn influences the student's need and ability profiles. Lack of either kind of potential inhibits learning the course content and will occasion some other outcome, desirable or undesirable. Figure 4–1 schematizes this process.

Crucial elements in this system are the specific needs and abilities. For want of better choice, some notion of student needs can be drawn from the validity literature just surveyed: the need for sufficient clarity of exposition, the need for positive regard, the need for appropriate motivation, and perhaps the need for breadth or integration. To these could be added the need for perceived meaningfulness of instructional goals and the need for at least perceived subject-matter competence on the part of the instructor. Abilities might be simply verbal and quantitative, or they might correspond to the Bloom or Guilford formulations given in chapter 1. Some if not all of these factors could be subdivided, especially the needs. Need for motivation, for example, might include intrinsic motivators (joy of learning, satisfaction with progress, fear of failure, etc.) and extrinsic motivators (praise, tests, immediate feedback, etc.).

Finally, the measure of the person-environment correspondence should be thoughtfully selected. Perfect correspondence on either the ability or need dimension is not specified by the model. On the contrary, perfect correspondence between, say, a profile of student needs and a profile of course rewards may lead to stagnation. Rather, the measure of correspondence should probably vary with the particular need or ability in question. The curvilinear, threshold, or double-threshold measures described above may be more appropriate than perfect correspondence.

Needed now are measures of student needs and course rewards, as well as suitable measures of student abilities and course demands. Construction of these measures can be expected to lead to refinements on all dimensions, and testing each correspondence should help uncover the important aspects of instruction which, when evaluated, should yield evaluations more meaningful in terms of student learning.

5 Generalizability

Almost everything is a sample of something. The students in a class are a sample of all students who will ever have taken the course. The faculty on a promotions committee are a sample of a greater number of faculty. The occasions on which a rating scale is administered are a sample of all possible occasions. And the conditions surrounding an evaluation are a sample of a universe of conditions.

Evaluative data, then, are always a sample from some universe of data.

Normally a decision maker—whether student, instructor, or administrator—is less interested in samples than in what those samples represent. To make inferences from samples to what they represent is to raise questions of generalizability.

In the abstract, the generalizability of a sample is the goodness with which it represents its universe. In the particular, the important feature of generalizability is that it directs attention to any differences in evaluations that might arise from sampling matters: differences due to the people whose opinions and observations are requested, differences due to the occasions of teaching that are evaluated, differences due to the circumstances surrounding the evaluation, and so forth.

Do different people give different evaluations? To approach this question, one should distinguish differences *across* groups of people—students, colleagues, administrators, alumni, self—and *within* each of these groups. A number of studies have compared one group's evaluation of a given instructor to another group's. Student ratings have been compared to an instructor's self-ratings (Davenport, 1944; Webb and Nolan, 1955; Blackburn and Clark, 1971; and especially Centra, 1972). The thrust of these studies seems to be that although students and instructors sometimes agree, and although self-ratings are sometimes more severe than student ratings, the general tendency is for instructors to rate themselves more favorably than their students do. It appears that students and instructor tend to agree about the *pattern* of the instructor's strengths and weaknesses (strongest point, next strongest, etc.) but to disagree about *level* (how strong are the strong points, how weak are the weak). Particular disagreement seems to occur on items relating to congruence between course objectives and actual teaching, the instructor's concern for and helpfulness toward student progress, and the students' feelings of freedom to ask questions and express

71

opinions. There is apparently no more disagreement for inexperienced teachers than experienced ones, but disagreement does seem to vary across curricula; for example, Centra's natural science instructors felt their courses were slower and that student effort was less than did their students, while his education and business, home economics, and nursing instructors judged pace to be faster and student effort to be greater than their students did. Greatest instructor-student agreement concerns how prepared the instructor was for class and the extent to which the course stimulated student interest.

Student ratings have also been compared to colleague and administrator ratings. (Students and colleagues: Knight, 1922; Broadman, 1928; Greene, 1933; Guthrie, 1949, 1954; Maslow and Zimmerman, 1956; and Aleamoni and Yimer, 1973. Students and administrators: Knight, 1922, Broadman, 1928; Greene, 1933; Bryan, 1937, Brookover, 1940; Webb and Nolan, 1955; and Costin, 1966.) When students and colleagues or administrators are asked to nominate, for example, "the ten best instructors," there is a high degree of similarity among the lists of names. But when more detailed comparisons are made—one group's ratings versus another's, say—the agreement seems to be low-to-moderate at best. In the latter case, correlations have been exclusively positive, often statistically significant, but rarely really strong. And most of these studies compared students' in-class *observations* with colleagues' or administrators' *inferences* about classroom activities based on their experiences with the instructor in other settings. The agreement noted might be due to certain general characteristics of the instructor that are observable in any setting—or to hearsay and the grapevine—while the disagreement might be more classroom-specific.

And student evaluations have been compared to alumni evaluations. It is sometimes suggested that alumni, with the presumed advantages of broader perspective, increased personal maturity, and greater real-world experience, are in a better position than current students to evaluate teachers. The two studies of this question seem to agree that there is little difference between evaluations by alumni and evaluations by current students; and when there is a difference the current students tend to give the more favorable evaluations. Centra (1974) used a measure of the "over-all effectiveness" of the instructor and found strong agreement between instructor rankings by students and by alumni of up to five year's standing. The agreement was stronger still with regard to exceptional teachers, both the "very good" and the "very poor." Drucker and Remmers (1951) used more specific questions. On six of the ten items that comprise the *Purdue Rating Scale for Instructors,* there were no differences in level of ratings between present and former students.[a] On three of the four items for which

---

[a] The no-difference items were: sympathetic attitude toward students, liberal and progressive attitude, presentation of subject, personal pecularities, personal appearance, and stimulation of intellectual curiosity.

a significant difference was found, the current students rated the instructor more favorably.[b] Only on "fairness in grading" did the alumni give more favorable ratings.

However, it is very difficult to interpret these data, for there is no way of knowing the extent and direction of any change that might have occurred in the instructor over the time periods involved. That is, five or ten year's experience might improve an instructor's teaching capabilities. If current students evaluate him more favorably than do former students, the difference could be simply a reflection of that change. If alumni and current-student evaluations are the same (and the instructor has in reality improved), then either the current students are too harsh or the former students are too lenient. The available studies, then, do not permit a firm conclusion regarding the generalizability of evaluations over current students and alumni, but the finding that current students tend to rate an instructor more favorably than former students do would be in keeping with a presumption that instructors improve with experience.

With regard to the generalizability of student evaluations to self, colleague, administrator, and alumni evaluations, then, it would seem in general that there is some similarity among data from the different sources but that the similarity is not strong enough to warrant substituting one set of data for another. Which data are the most accurate descriptions of the instructor is a matter of reliability (see chapter 3).

Differences among information from different people can also be examined within groups. A great deal of attention has been devoted to the relationship between student evaluations and student characteristics,[c] that is, differences across groups of students variously categorized. The importance of these studies can be illustrated by a hypothetical example. Suppose there were a consistent relationship between student evaluations and, say, student sex, such that women students rate instructors more favorably than do men students. Two identical instructors teaching the identical course would then receive different evaluations if one were teaching all men and the other all women. The shifting proportions of men and women would ipso facto change the resulting evaluations, and any sampling of student evaluations would have to take into account this particular source of ratings bias.

The most frequently studied student characteristics seem to fall into three classes: demographics (such as sex and year in school), ability, and motivation. Studies of the relationship between student evaluations and

---

[b] Instructor's interest in subject, sense of proportion and humor, self reliance and confidence.

[c] de Wolf (1974), for example, lists seventy-six student characteristics that have been studied as predictors of student evaluations, ranging from age to amount of travel experience!

74

student sex (e.g., Bowman, 1934; Bryan, 1937, Davenport, 1944; Henrikson, 1949; Bendig, 1952; Lovell and Haner, 1955; Doyle, 1972; and Doyle and Whitely, 1974) and year in school (e.g., Guthrie, 1927; Bendig, 1952; Lovell and Haner, 1955; Doyle and Whitely, 1974) have found scattered relationships but indicate as a general trend that these student characteristics are unrelated to evaluations. When relationships are found, they are usually such that their influence is trivial (Doyle and Whitely, 1974).

The relationship between student ability and student evaluations has quite often been examined. Ability measures have sometimes been achievement test scores like the Scholastic Aptitude Test; often they have been grades. Some studies have found no relationship between ability and evaluations.[d] Other studies have found significant relationships, usually positive but sometimes even negative.[e] These seemingly contrary results can be explained by an interpretation first offered more than 25 years ago (Remmers, Martin, and Elliott, 1949): Confronted with a class heterogeneous in ability, an instructor can gear the course to the quicker, average or slower students. This choice will determine the relationship between ability and evaluations. For example, if the instructor directs his teaching to the brighter students, these students should be relatively more satisfied and the correlation between ability and ratings will be positive. Conversely, if the instructor teaches to the slower students, these students will be more satisfied—and the brighter ones less so—and the correlation will be negative. Elliott (1950) provides data that substantiate this interpretation. Fortunately, perhaps, it does not seem necessary routinely to determine the ability of students to whom an instructor gears his teaching, for even when relationships are found between ability and ratings, the relative amount of influence of ability (like the influence of sex and year in school) on the data is minimal (see Treffinger and Feldhusen, 1970; Rayder, 1968; Doyle and Whitely, 1974).[f]

---

[d] Staraak, 1934; Smeltzer and Harter, 1934; Krous, 1934; Heilman and Armentrout, 1936; Bryan, 1937; Detchen, 1940; Blum, 1936; Bendig. 1953; Cohen and Humphries, 1960; Eckert, 1950; Garverick and Carter, 1962; Guthrie, 1949, 1954; Hudelson, 1951; Remmers, 1928, 1930, 1939, 1960; Russell, 1951; Voeks and French, 1960; Doyle and Whitely, 1974.

[e] Anikeef, 1953; Caffrey, 1969; Echandia, 1964; Rayder, 1968; Elliott, 1950; Rubenstein and Mitchell, 1970; Russell and Bendig, 1953; Spencer, 1968; Root, 1931; Stewart and Malpass, 1966; Treffinger and Feldhusen, 1970; Walker, 1969; and Weaver, 1960.

[f] Although grades are to a large extent indexes of student ability, it is perhaps somewhat dangerous to treat grades and achievement test scores simultaneously. The question of any influence of grades on ratings should not be overlooked. It is entirely possible that in some situations grades can influence ratings or, by the same token, that ratings can influence grades. Students can rate an instructor harshly or generously because of the grades they receive (or anticipate) and instructors can grade

However, it sometimes is important to examine the ratings of subgroups of students separately. Since by definition reliable evaluations will reflect substantive differences in people's perceptions of the treatment they receive, to the extent that instruction is very different for different groups of students, the evaluations from these students should be considered separately (e.g., cross tabulated). For example, ratings from graduate students in a course taught primarily for undergraduates may well be different from the undergraduates' ratings. And men's evaluations of a course on sex roles taught from a feminist point of view may well be different from women's evaluations of the same course. In such cases, evaluations cannot always be expected to generalize across student groups.

Another set of student characteristics is motivation-related: whether or not the course was required, how much the students liked the subject matter of the course, and, for that matter, how much the students liked the instructor as a person. A number of studies have compared ratings from students for whom the course was a requirement with ratings from those for whom it was not. Gage (1961), Lovell and Haner (1955), and Cohen and Humphreys (1960) all found ratings less favorable when the course was required. Heileman and Armentrout (1936) found no difference. Doyle and Whitely (1974) found a tendency toward a relationship between a course's being required or elective and students' ratings of how stimulating it was but generally no relationship between ratings and this index of student motivation.

One reason for the minor inconsistency in these results may be the fact that asking whether or not a course is required does not produce a clear-cut separation of students according to motivation. Some students for whom the course was required may have *wanted* to take it anyway, and some for whom it was an elective may have been obliged to take it for other reasons (e.g., scheduling). A better question might be something like, "How much did you want to take this course?"; but no study of the relationship between ratings and responses to such a question seems yet to have appeared.

It is also not clear that the instructor's behavior is the same in courses that are required for significant numbers of students as in courses freely entered by most of the students. Required courses are often beginning courses that are the favorites neither of students nor instructors. The be-

---

a class harshly or generously because of the ratings he receives (or anticipates). However, general research on the relationship of grades and ratings will not identify these situation-specific occurrences. Rather, the possibility of bias of these sorts should be considered during the interpretation of particular sets of evaluative information. One should expect grades to have little influence on ratings unless the grades given are drastically incommensurate with the grades expected. And even in this case, the greatest effect should be on ratings describing "fairness in grading," although some spill-over to other ratings might be encountered.

havioral ramifications of an instructor's unwillingness to teach such a course may well account for the relationship found. Or student unwillingness may make it difficult for an instructor to teach as well as he might, which could also account for differences in ratings. In any event, at least until the state of affairs is more clearly understood, one should probably consider information not generalizable across students who wanted to take the course and those who did not.

Students' stated liking for the subject matter of the course appears to be related to some kinds of ratings but not others. At least in the one available study (Doyle and Whitely, 1974), ratings of over-all course and instructor effectiveness—but not overall teaching *ability*—did correlate with liking for the subject matter. It would appear that "liked subject matter" is one component of an effective course, but that "teaching ability" can be rated without reference to liking for the material. Ratings on items like "got you interested in the course" and "made you want to take more courses in the area" also correlate with liking for the subject matter, which seems entirely reasonable. But ratings of the instructor's expositional skills (clarity of communication, etc.) and attitudes toward students (respect, genuine, etc.) are apparently unrelated to students' liking for the subject. Moreover, an examination of the ratings from the class as a whole (i.e., as summarized by the mean), indicates no relationship between liking for the material and any rating item. Apparently computing the mean cancels out individual students' likes and dislikes. Thus liking for the subject does not appear to be a source of bias in ratings of general teaching ability.

The situation is similar with regard to liking for the instructor as a person. As far as specific instructor traits and behaviors are concerned, liking for the person relates to ratings of the instructor's attitudes toward students but not to any other ratings. With regard to over-all evaluations, liking for the person seems to be a component of "over-all effectiveness" but is not related to ratings of general teaching ability. Again, the relationships seem appropriate and provide no reason to anticipate bias in the ratings. So there is no need, at least on the basis of these data, to separate evaluations of general teaching ability of people who liked the course material or person from those who did not.

There appear to have been no studies of the possible influence of colleague or administrator characteristics on evaluations, nor any regarding the personal characteristics of instructors who might tend to over- or underrate themselves.

Does it matter which occasions of teaching are evaluated? If "occasions of teaching" refers to types of courses, e.g., pure lecture courses, lecture/ discussion courses, and discussion or seminar courses, then it does appear to make a difference. It seems that discussion courses are rated somewhat more favorably than courses with a heavy lecture component.[g] Doyle, Bejar, and Whitely (1974) found differences on most kinds of rating items —instructor characteristics, reading materials, how much students felt they learned, and even general teaching ability. (No difference was found on liking for the subject matter.) Now, whether these differences should be considered legitimate or not is not so easily determined. There is no satisfactory way of determining whether the differences rise from, say, the fact that students just like to have the opportunity to talk in class (or do not like just to sit and take notes) and therefore let that preference bias their ratings or if the instructor is really different in discussion courses than in lectures or if the better instructors simply happen to teach discussion courses. Since the ratings are technically reliable and as such should reflect any real instructional differences, and since subject matter liking did not change across type of course, there is some reason to believe that the ratings describe real differences. But, legitimate or not, the differences are there, and so evaluations of instruction in highly different types of courses should be examined separately. Otherwise instructors who teach lecture courses may find themselves disadvantaged.

If "occasions of teaching" means which offering of a particular type of course should be evaluated, data will be of little help. Rather, common sense should make the decision. If an experienced instructor is teaching the same courses he has taught for some time, and if he has made no really major changes in these courses, it probably does not matter which offering is selected. (This assumes that there are no extenuating circumstances that might cause one offering to be more favorably rated than another, for instance that the students in one offering had all been free to choose the course and in another had all been required to take it.) But if an instructor has just completely revised a course or is teaching it for the first time, his evaluations there might be expected to be less favorable than in another more established course. A thorough evaluation should portray a representation of his teaching, and so one should pay attention to those courses in which evaluations are most likely to portray the instructor as he typically is (particularly in terms of the kinds of courses he will be teaching in the future).

If "occasions of teaching" means which session within a given course offering should be evaluated, the generalizability of information depends on the consistency of the instructor's behavior. Generalizability here is less likely to be a problem with student ratings, since at least the implicit instruction to students is to describe the instructor as he usually is, than it is

---

[g] E.g., Clark and Keller, in Eckert and Keller, 1954; Heilman and Armentrout, 1936; Lovell and Haner, 1955. But see Goodhartz, 1948, Guthrie, 1954, and Solomon, 1966, for a finding of no relationship between evaluations and class size.

with colleagues or administrator ratings, which even under the best of circumstances involve attendance at only a few class sessions. Retest reliability studies of student evaluation (see chapter 3) can be interpreted to mean that when the evaluation occurs is probably not particularly important, so long as (1) the students are asked to rate typical performance; (2) they have had sufficient opportunity to observe the instructor; and (3) the evaluations do not take place at the same time as special events like holidays, perhaps, or examinations that might influence the data. There are no data available that indicate exactly at what point students have formed a dependable picture of the instructor, although it is quite clear that impressions begin to form as early as the first class session (Bejar and Doyle, 1974b). The literature is even more sparse with regard to bias from proximity to examinations and durability of impressions after a course is over. However, common sense may answer these questions as well as any data. Evaluations for administrative decisions require descriptions of representative samples of instructor behavior. Such evaluations before at least a week or two of experience with the instructor are extremely risky; a whole term's experience is certainly preferable. Instructor-improvement evaluations, however, need not to the same extent describe representative behavior. Such evaluations could very properly occur at *any* time during the course. Indeed, instructional improvement evaluations should be almost continuous, though they need not more than occasionally involve formal devices like questionnaires and rating scales. Moreover, there is much to be said for early evaluations that might enable the students who provided the data to share its benefits. Evaluations should probably not be requested with examinations, for they then would constitute a special imposition on the students and would run the risk of bias from positive or negative emotions surrounding the examination. And there should rarely be any reason for delaying evaluations more than a few days after a term. Not only will recollections fade, but response rate problems may become severe.

There is no basis for a conclusion about the generalizability of colleague and administrator ratings within a given course offering. Perhaps the most one can say is that the representativeness or generalizability of these evaluations will always be open to challenge.

Do circumstances surrounding an evaluation affect the data? Some do. With regard to the instructor's presence or absence during the evaluation, the student evaluation literature is again sparse. But the social psychology literature supplies abundant evidence that perception—and therefore ratings—can be influenced by the social context (e.g., Schachter, in Glass, 1967). Thus an instructor's demeanor immediately before and during an evaluation might unduly affect the ratings, and the instructor's absence from the classroom might be conducive to more representative evaluations. However, if the instructor maintains his customary demeanor—aided, perhaps, by a set of standardized instructions—there would be no compelling reason for his absence.[h]

Available data do not support the widely held notion that ratings will be different if students identify themselves rather than remain anonymous. Although there is a tendency for raw ratings to be slightly more favorable from identified students, the effect is not enough to make the means either statistically or practically different (Sharon, 1970). But there are compelling reasons why evaluations should be anonymous (or at least confidential), namely, that anonymity and confidentiality preclude the possibility than an occasional unscrupulous instructor retaliate against individual students, and, in hopefully more typical situations, that students may be somewhat more willing to participate in the evaluation if their anonymity is assured.

The anonymity of colleagues and administrators who might visit a classroom can hardly be preserved, and the extent to which this identification might influence evaluations is an open question. Centra (1974) did point out that colleague ratings are reminiscent of self ratings in terms of leniency effect.

The known purpose of the evaluation also seems to influence the data (see Sharon, 1970; and Sharon and Bartlett, 1969). When students believed that their ratings would go to a departmental committee for personnel purposes, the evaluations were more favorable than when they believed the data were intended for research purposes only. And when students believed they would be asked to justify their ratings in a face-to-face situation with the instructor, the evaluations were similarly more favorable. So the stated purposes of the evaluation does make a difference, and information gathered under different conditions should not be interchanged or compared. Since conducting different evaluations for different purposes would seldom be efficient, a better solution might be to advise the students either that *no* rating will be used for administrative purposes or that *any* rating *might* be so used (whichever is the case) and thus equalize conditions across courses by taking the most conservative approach. Some people legitimately advocate that a statement be printed on evaluation forms indicating which items—e.g., over-all ratings—may be used for personnel purposes and asking for special care and frankness in responses to those items.

From this survey of the generalizability literature, it becomes quite clear that a number of different factors, especially those that concern student willingness to be enrolled in the course and certain circumstances surrounding the evaluation itself, may introduce some bias into the data. Some ways of coping with these biases have already been mentioned. Others will be described in the following chapter.

---

[h] It should be noted that some institutions are beginning to report instances of falsification of data by faculty and have therefore established proctor systems.

6 Utility

The purpose of this chapter is to describe how student evaluations and other kinds of instructional evaluations might appropriately be used for various purposes, given their reliability, validity, and generalizability.

Can student evaluations be used for rank, pay, tenure, and similar personnel decisions about individual faculty? The social ethic proposed in an earlier chapter indicates that the greater potential a decision holds for harm to individual faculty, the more rigorous must be the data upon which the decision is based. Consequently, rank, pay, and tenure decisions require a very high degree of reliability, and they must be appropriately meaningful. Research on the reliability of student ratings points quite clearly to the conclusion that ratings obtained from typically responsible students on rating scales constructed to professional standards regularly achieve a very high degree of reliability. Especially in comparison to other data, but also in absolute terms, student ratings do seem to be of sufficient precision to be used in personnel decisions. Colleague evaluations, and student evaluations gathered on less well constructed instruments, may or may not be reliable enough for personnel use, depending on the instrument, the people, and one's particular standards of reliability.[a] Since there seldom should be any reason that student rating instruments of less than professional quality should have to be used, given that measurement specialists are available on most campuses and permission to use well researched forms is quite easily obtained, the question becomes one of the appropriateness of *colleague* ratings in personnel decisions. Because lack of opportunity to observe the instruction they are asked to evaluate is probably the factor that most limits the reliability of colleague evaluations, a reasonable conclusion might be that colleague evaluations of teaching are appropriate only to the extent that colleagues have had the opportunity to observe the teaching. Even with this condition satisfied, however, the relatively sparse knowledge about colleague evaluations dictates that in case of disagreement between student and colleague evaluations, the burden of proof rests with the latter. (The

---

[a] One could argue that student ratings *must* be used in the instructional component of personnel decisions. Since such decisions must be made, and since student ratings are generally more reliable than, and at least as valid as, any other measure of classroom instruction, it follows that student ratings must be primary data in these decisions.

fact that self ratings are not likely to be persuasive in personnel decisions does not mean that the instructor should have to remain passive throughout the procedure. Indeed there is much to argue that it should be largely his own responsibility to outline the evaluation, to marshall evidence of his effectiveness, and to rebut negative evaluations so far as he is able.)

Probably the most appropriate question to ask students for personnel purposes is simply "How would you rate the general teaching ability of this instructor?" [b] for this item is valid to the extent of its reliability (i.e., it means what its words say) and it also tends to infer qualities and outcomes that many would consider germane, such as expositional skill, stimulation of ideas and thinking, motivation of interest in the subject matter, and some kinds of tested learning. The explicit inclusion in personnel decisions of specific instructor characteristics (attitudes toward students, expositional skills, etc.) should be decided on the basis of how willing people are to accept those qualities as their definition of good teaching. Sometimes these kinds of information do not add significantly to the general rating and may simply result in information overload. Other times this specific information helps define the students' conception of good teaching. Including items that relate to matters not completely under the instructor's control—reading materials and student outcomes, for example—requires that the decision maker determine the extent to which the instructor is really responsible for the quality of these aspects of instruction. These are probably the kinds of student evaluations least justifiable for personnel purposes, although they too can help define the basic "general teaching ability" rating. All things considered, the single general item stated above is probably by itself the best item for personnel decisions. Ratings on this item could constitute the primary data, and if there is any reason to doubt the general rating other data could be appealed to, such as specific instructor ratings, evaluative narratives, and explanations from the instructor. However, a very strong case should be required of these supplementary data before they are given precedence over the general teaching ability rating.

(It should be noted that the emphasis here is on the evaluation of classroom instruction. Other important aspects of teaching, such as choice of objectives and knowledge relevant to the course, can be evaluated by colleagues and administrators as well as by students. Here no group seems especially distinguished by lack of opportunity to observe. While one might be tempted to challenge students' estimates of an instructor's knowledge, Elliott's (1950) paper does indicate at least a significant relationship between student ratings of instructor knowledge and knowledge demonstrated by the instructor on an achievement test. Analogous data do not seem to exist for colleague or administrator ratings.)

---

[b] Perhaps on a 6- or 7-point "excellent" to "very poor" scale.

In the reporting of these evaluations, the mean is probably the most appropriate statistic for personnel decisions, although the decision maker should examine the frequency distribution to see how well the mean represents the opinion of the whole class. Means of particular subgroups of students—e.g., majors versus nonmajors—might be examined separately, especially if there is reason to suspect that different groups of students might give sharply different evaluations of the instructor. In case of disagreement, the specific circumstances of the course—e.g., for whom especially it was taught—should help in the weighting of the different groups' evaluations.

Finally, a certain amount of control over the conditions of the evaluation should be maintained. First, the general rating should be examined separately for each principal kind of course the instructor teaches and should be weighted in terms of the instructor's responsibility for those kinds of courses. Second, evaluations should be accumulated over time, especially in the case of less experienced instructors and less established courses, in order that any patterns of improvement can be noted. Third, evaluation procedures should be reasonably standardized. Instructors should probably all be in or all out of the classroom during student evaluations (and, in the latter case especially, standardized instructions should be read to the students—without benefit of *ad libitum* commentary). The purpose of the evaluation should be stated identically to all raters, colleagues as well as students. All ratings should be confidential if not anonymous. Student evaluations should probably not be gathered just before or after examinations. And, finally, people charged with interpreting the data should be informed of the following circumstances: whether the course was required of a preponderance of students; when and under what conditions the evaluation took place; and whether, generally speaking, there is any reason to distrust a particular set of ratings. In short, personnel ratings especially must always be interpreted in context and with judgment.

Can student evaluations and other evaluations be legitimately used to help improve instruction? Again the answer depends on the reliability and validity of the particular data. With the exceptions of (a) individual students' gain scores on achievement tests and (b) statements about classroom instruction from people who have not had the opportunity to observe that instruction, all of the information to which the last three chapters have referred are probably reliable enough to make a contribution to the improvement of teaching.

That evaluative feedback regarding specific course and instructor characteristics can result in changes in those characteristics seems clearly to be the case. Although Miller (1971) and Centra (1972) found that simply reporting student ratings to instructors could not be counted on to lead to improved ratings a few months later, Root (1931), Aleamoni (1974), and

McKeachie (1974) all found that when guidance in some form—counsel from a master teacher or extensive narrative evaluations from students—accompanies the evaluation results, change does indeed occur. Centra (1972) also noted that instructors are most likely to change when student ratings are considerably less favorable than self-ratings and that at least two semester's experience with student evaluations may be required before the change is noticeable. These studies, along with one or two qualifications, lead to a rather obvious conclusion: Given that (a) the evaluated qualities are changeable, (b) that the instructor wants to change, and (c) that the evaluative statements are worded to provide explicit guidance regarding the desired change and/or that instructional resources are available to help with the desired change, then student evaluations and probably most other kinds of diagnostic evaluations can lead to changes in instruction.

Appraising the appropriateness of these changes is a matter of validity. Since reliable evaluations mean what their words say, if the wording of evaluations reflects sound judgment about what constitutes good teaching in a particular course, then changes of the kinds suggested by the evaluations are in those terms appropriate. It is not possible given the present state of knowledge to state definitely that a given change will result in more or better learning on the part of students. There is some basis in the research literature, and considerable basis in common sense, for the position that needed improvements in expositional skills may lead to increased learning for many students. It may also be that too many demands are placed on instructor traits and behaviors. Perhaps there is no reason to expect that the greater one's expositional skills the more one's students will learn. Perhaps the instructor's task in this regard is simply to communicate material with sufficient clarity that the material can be understood, that the occasion for learning can be established (See Figure 4–1). A similar situation may hold for attitudes toward students. Neither the research literature nor common sense provides much basis for expecting a linear relationship between tested learning and an instructor's attitude toward students. Again it may be that the instructor's attitudes should simply not be destructive, should not so offend that the occasion for learning is diminished.[c] So, requisite knowledge along with adequacy in these two regards may define the adequate teacher, and these factors plus effectiveness in stimulating or motivating students may define the exceptional teacher. Until these and other substantive and methodological issues are resolved, the cautious person will rely on good judgment, tempered by these sparse research findings, as the basis for appraising the appropriateness of instructional change.

Instructional–improvement data can be gathered in many ways (see

---

[c] To the extent that role modeling for students is important, however, more positive attitudes may be desirable.

chapter 2). When rating scales are used, the data should be reported as frequency distributions, the number of respondents choosing each of the different alternatives. Whenever there is reason to expect considerable divergence of opinion among groups of students, the evaluations should be tabulated separately for the different groups.[d] But rating scales are generally only somewhat useful for improving instruction; the range of questions in most rating scales can point out general areas of strength and weakness, but the very breadth of these instruments often operates against useful specificity. The cafeteria approach and its variations allow for greater specificity. But whenever narrative evaluations—spoken as well as written—are at all possible, they should be used at least to supplement rating scales.

While it has been emphasized that student outcome measures should not be used in personnel evaluations because people should not be evaluated with respect to matters beyond their control, outcome measures may be appropriate for course improvement purposes. Course examinations can certainly inform instructors about student attainment of certain kinds of instructional goals. Students' goal-attainment ratings may be similarly useful, especially for the kinds of goal attainment that are difficult to tap with course examinations. Hoyt (1973; see also Hoyt, in Sockloff, 1973) describes an instrument that combines students' self-evaluations in goal-attainment terms with general and specific ratings of course and instructor characteristics. And a kind of cafeteria system employing both trait and outcome ratings as well as narrative evaluations could provide exceptionally useful instruments for course improvement.

Finally, can student evaluations be legitimately used to help other students choose courses and instructors? Again, the reliability of the data seems sufficient to the purpose. The evident and inferential validity of overall items and the evident (but probably not the inferential) validity of specific items also seem sufficient for this purpose, especially if the data are reported separately for different student types. But two kinds of problems still exist. First, this use of evaluative data differs from the other principal uses in that these data become public matters (e.g., published in handbooks) and therefore are not so controllable as data the accessible only to the instructor, faculty committees, and administrators. This lack of control means that the qualifications, rebuttals, and other matters that are extremely important to the interpretation of these data are not likely to be includable (and if includable are not likely to be effective). Moreover, once published the data cannot be recalled, and past issues, say, of a student

---

[d] One should not expect that cross tabulation will remove all of the variability from a set of ratings. Not only is it frequently very difficult to determine the basis for grouping the students, but only some of the variability is due to legitimate difference of opinion. Ratings error—leniency, stringency, carelessness, and so forth—also contributes to variability.

handbook are taken as indicators of the current quality of instruction, regardless of whether the instructor has changed for the better or the worse since publication. If these problems of control and currentness can be resolved (say by making the data available only to a trained advising staff that would help students interpret the information and see to it that out-of-date data are removed from circulation, then a general, evaluative question might be appropriate for this purpose. As with evaluation for the other purpose, some cross tabulation of data by student types may be desirable. Even then, however, the advising system may be open to the criticism that it tends to emphasize less important factors at the expense of more important ones. That is, critics could legitimately argue that the most important matters in course selection are, first, that the area of study be the proper one in terms of the student's academic, vocational, and personal interests and needs, and only then should one attend to the particulars of course and instructor. It seems likely too, that the most useful data for advising purposes are nonevaluative. Perhaps the greatest deficiency in most advising systems is the lack of detailed and accurate information about the course—its objectives, for whom it is intended, its content, its instructional procedures, and so forth. Effort and resources may be more effectively expended in the direction of providing students with dependable information of these types than in gathering and publically reporting the detailed instructor evaluations often found in student handbooks.[e]

In summary, then, provided that the data are gathered carefully, reported appropriately, and interpreted judiciously, student evaluations appear able to make a useful contribution to personnel decisions, course improvement, and, possibly, to student advising.

---

[e] An appealing alternative to specific ratings for course improvement and for advising students may eventually be the needs/satisfiers model described in chapter 4. At the present time, however, the formulation is not refined enough for other than experimental use.

**Part III
Implementation**

7

Some Principles and an Agenda

No general presentation can effectively treat the institution-specific details of establishing an instructional evaluation system. But it can suggest some principles that seem to make for the smoother implementation of such systems and point out some of the practical decisions that will have to be made.

General Principles

Evaluation systems should be participating, reasonable, sensitive, and constructive. Participating means that everyone plays a part in the development, utilization, and refinement of the system. The roles of different groups of people in the evaluation process vary according to the nature of the institution and its traditions, but certain roles seem to predominate for certain groups. The principal role of trustees and higher level administrators is usually to encourage and to fund the system. These people can effectively facilitate evaluation by urging it as a matter of institutional policy and perhaps by establishing some very general guidelines depicting the purposes and parameters of the system. They can also facilitate evaluation by taking its results seriously, for example by confirming decisions made on the basis of evaluative information and challenging decisions made without such information. They can direct financial support not only toward the creation and operation of the system, but also toward faculty development and reward. Resources over and above those that support evaluation should be made available to help and to encourage faculty to improve their teaching, funds to support a center for instructional development, for example, or to purchase instructional resources, or to send faculty to workshops on improving teaching, or to bring instructional consultants to the campus, and funds to reward instructional excellence and significant progress toward excellence. (It may be as important to reward the less effective instructor for substantial improvement as it is to reward the excellent instructor for continuing excellence.)

It is usually a fact, however, that the smooth implementation of an evaluation system is *not* enhanced by mandates from trustees and ad-

89

ministrators, especially when the procedural details of the system are mandated.

One of the principal roles of students is to cooperate with the evaluation system by conscientiously filling out student evaluation forms. This most students do. But one of the frustrations of people who are actively involved in faculty evaluation is that sometimes significant numbers of students decline to provide evaluations and others seem to treat the forms with a mixture of humor and contempt. Certainly a substantial part of student reluctance to participate is due to the forms themselves, which are often ill-conceived and trivial; some is due to the evaluation system proper, which usually fails to communicate to students the importance of their cooperation; and some to the occasional faculty member who, perhaps out of self-consciousness or defensiveness or perhaps out of principle, indicates that student evaluations are formalities that must be tolerated but that in reality deserve and will receive no serious consideration. And some student reluctance is due to the fact that a number of students "just can't be bothered." An evaluation system is just as unlikely to win the support of all students as it is to win the support of all faculty, but involving more students more actively and visibly in the system can be expected to increase general student participation if for no other reason than that student-perceived weaknesses in instruments and procedures could then be more easily identified and remedied. Thus students should sit on committees charged with the creation, operation, and refinement of the evaluation system.

The role of faculty, in cooperation or at least conjunction with students and administrators, is to play the major part in the construction of the system, particularly with respect to policy and procedural matters, to monitor the system and make constructive changes, and to support the system and urge colleagues and students and administrators and trustees to do the same. Supporting the system means more than not trying to subvert it; it means making efforts to see that good information is collected, that the information is judiciously interpreted, and that decisions made on the basis of the information are carried out. A special role belongs to faculty who are the subjects of an evaluation. As noted earlier, they should not be only passive; rather they should see to it that the evaluation is an accurate and realistic description of their effectiveness and potential. Accordingly, besides cooperating with the data gathering procedures, they should actively provide information about their specific circumstances: special goals they are trying to help their students achieve, particular weaknesses they are trying to remedy, attempted innovations that proved unsuccessful, and any other special circumstances that might temper or qualify the evaluation.

The active and conscientious involvement of people from each of these groups, each in his own way, defines a participating system. And participation should make it more likely that a system is reasonable, sensitive, and constructive.

A reasonable evaluation system is one that does not do violence to common sense. Common sense dictates that no data, no system, will ever be perfect, but that selected data carefully collected and interpreted can provide a basis for better personnel decisions, better course improvement decisions, and better decisions about course selection. To claim or demand more, or to settle for less, is not reasonable. Common sense also dictates that all of these decisions are too complicated and too important to be made impersonally. Therefore "evaluations" from whatever source should be considered *information,* and whatever decision is to be made should be made on the basis of thoughtful *evaluation of that information,* never mechanistically, never without the advantage of knowing as much as possible about specific circumstances. Thus efforts to devise computer programs, tables of cut-off points, and other devices that remove the burden of evaluation from people are not reasonable. In the same vein, all but the most capricious objections to evaluation deserve serious attention, and merely dismissing or out-voting reasonable objections does nothing to make the system a more effective one.

Evaluation is sensitive when it recognizes the complexity and the consequences of evaluation. Glib pronouncements about the goodness of a system or an instrument or a particular set of data, dismissal of bonafide objections to evaluation, mechanistic decisions, lack of attention to individual circumstances, lack of opportunity for rebuttal to say nothing of grievance—none of these is characteristic of a sensitive system. Moreover, the absence of these negative characteristics does not by itself make a system sensitive. For a truly sensitive evaluation program realizes that evaluation is not just an end in itself but also a means for improving teaching. Therefore, a sensitive system is also a constructive one.

Constructive means that the evaluation program has a faculty development component. The need for this provision is clear in the case of diagnostic self-improvement evaluations. Diagnostic ratings are constructive only to the extent that the ratings items or narrative responses indicate what improvements seem warranted, what steps an instructor might take to improve his ratings and his teaching. But rank, pay, and especially tenure evaluations should also be constructive, that is, they should inform faculty of the reasons for any unfavorable ratings and should outline steps that should lead to improvement. Since most evaluations—i.e., sets of evaluative information—are not by themselves really sufficient to this task, a system should at least provide lists of various kinds of instructional resources available to faculty. Better still, it should incorporate the listing of resources into the evaluation report, perhaps in the form of computer-generated letters to individual instructors that summarize rating reports and suggest steps that might be taken to strengthen specific weaknesses (see Doyle and Bejar, 1973), perhaps in the form of self-teaching packages about instructional improvement, perhaps in the form of lists of faculty who are willing to help other faculty become better teachers. Best of all, perhaps, would be provision of a visible and credible faculty development service stocked with publications on improving teaching[a] and staffed by people whose primary charge is the improvement of instruction.

Two final principles are that the evaluation system should be visible and credible. Visibility is important in order that faculty can take advantage of services offered, both evaluative and developmental, and so that faculty, administrators, trustees, and students will recognize and be more likely to fulfill their roles. Visibility can be achieved quite quickly through announcements, newsletters, and the like, and relatively slowly by simply being available and working with individuals and units. Both approaches to visibility are effective. The need for credibility is almost self-explanatory; the system will not survive if the people associated with it are not seen as trustworthy. Credibility applies not only to competence in the field of evaluation but also to the goodness of policies and straightforwardness of operating procedures. Every effort should be taken, for example, to assure that clerical errors in data processing are avoided. And if evaluative information is obtained for nonpublic use and assurance given to that effect, then under no circumstances should that policy be violated, regardless of any faculty committees, chairmen, deans, vice presidents, trustees, or student leaders who might insist on access to the data. Similarly, any information stored, whether in the form of reports or questionnaires or computer cards, should be stored securely; in fact, it is often a good idea to remove identification from data storage, or at least to code it in such a way that individual attribution is impossible. A final aspect of credibility is the courage to acknowledge that systems and instruments are imperfect and that much remains to be learned. Defensiveness about one's pet evaluation program is not compatible with credibility.

Points of Decision

Regardless of where the impetus for an evaluation program comes from, faculty or students or administrators or trustees, the task of designing the system usually and appropriately falls on some committee or task force.

---

[a] Some such publications are McKeachie (1969), MacKenzie, Eraut, and Jones (1970), and Astin, Comstock, Epperson, Greeley, Katz, and Kauffman (1974), and Freedman (1973).

This task force needs to consider many things. These last few pages are an attempt to list and comment on some of those things.

Purpose of the Evaluation Program

It should be clear now that defining the purpose of the evaluation is one of the most important single steps in the development of any evaluation system because so many subsequent decisions will depend on purpose. (See chapter 1.)

Conceptualization

The conceptualization of evaluation provided by Figures 1–2 and 1–3 can reduce some of the initial confusion a task force usually faces and can define a part of the task force's agenda. The sources of evaluative information deserve special attention, particularly in terms of which are the best sources of information about the various aspects of instruction. Chapters 3, 4, and 5 speak in some detail to the comparative rigor of data from different sources.

Instrumentation

Selection or construction of rating scales and questionnaires is usually a primary concern of any task force on instructional evaluation. Chapter 2 describes a variety of student evaluation forms. (See also the Appendix.)

The temptation usually arises to construct one's own student evaluation instrument. To build a good instrument, however, is a time-consuming and very costly undertaking. Unless there is truly a compelling reason to develop one's own form, the better choice is to adopt an existing one or to adapt it to one's needs.[b] If undertaken at all, construction of one's own instrument should involve measurement specialists, preferably specialists in the evaluation of instruction, at least on a consulting basis. The so-called armchair approach chosen by many committees will seldom result in a technically sound instrument and may well leave one ethically if not legally vulnerable. A special note should be made with regard to the cafeteria systems (p. 28). Ideally, all items available through the system

---

[b] Most well researched forms are protected by statutory copyright and should therefore not be used or modified without authorization. Many copyright holders, however, are willing to authorize use or adaptation of their instruments.

should be prescreened for basic technical strength; in the very least, items to be used in personnel decisions should receive special research attention, and those items only should be used as basic data in personnel decisions. (See chapter 6.)

Application

Once the instruments are selected, decisions need to be reached about who is to be evaluated, when, and under what circumstances. (See chapters 4 and 6.) Who is to be evaluated and when is defined by the need for evaluative information. For example, there is generally a greater need for personnel evaluations of untenured faculty than of full professors, especially, perhaps, when the time for the tenure decision is approaching. An instructor may need self-improvement evaluations more the first few times a course is offered or after a major revision than when the course is well established. And an instructor whose evaluations are consistently favorable should have less need for information than might less favorably rated colleagues. Self-improvement evaluation, should be a continuing process but need not always involve formal devices like questionnaires and rating scales. It is usually not necessary, and it is often not a good idea, to ask all students to rate all their instructors every term. Evaluation of this sort is uneconomical, and students and faculty alike will soon tire of the process, so such a program of evaluation may be in the long run self-defeating. But just as one should not require universal evaluation, one should not prohibit it. A program that insists that evaluations be collected during a particular week and at no other time is not in keeping with the instructional improvement purpose of evaluations.

Formal self-improvement student evaluations are perhaps better done relatively early in the course so the students can share the benefits of the evaluation and be available to help interpret and clarify it. Personnel-decision student evaluations should wait until the students have experienced at least a representation portion of the course, if not the entirety of the course. Many faculty find it useful to ask for narrative evaluations rather early in a term, and summary ratings rather late. The narratives are used for instructional improvement, the ratings for personnel purposes. When multiple evaluations are asked, however, it becomes especially important to enlist the cooperation of students by indicating one's need for, and the importance of, those data and perhaps by summarizing to the students the results of the evaluation and the changes proposed.

Certain circumstances surrounding the collection of evaluative ratings appear to influence those ratings. The announced purpose of the evaluation is one of those factors. It is possible that other factors too might influence

faculty teaching similar courses, can provide information useful for interpreting one's own ratings. Even simple averages of ratings of similar courses within a department may be helpful. However, it should be recognized that norms will at most be approximate guidelines, since even the most carefully executed norming study will be unable to control all factors that might influence the ratings a particular instructor receives in a particular course. Moreover, norms may create some morale problems, since by definition half of the faculty will receive below average ratings. In this regard, normative interpretations of ratings should not be confused with absolute interpretations, i.e., interpretations based on the wording of the evaluative questions and response alternatives and without any comparisons to other people's ratings. If in absolute terms, for example, most of the teachers in an institution are excellent, then to be below average may still be very good. Conversely, if most of the teachers are terrible, to be above average may be only very poor. The question of normative versus absolute interpretation is a policy matter that, especially for personnel decision evaluations, should be settled early. The basic questions are: If good is below average, is good good enough? And if poor is above average, is poor good enough? The deciding factors will include the expectations and priorities of the institution, its ability to attract excellent teaching faculty, and the job market.

A final consideration with respect to data processing concerns storage of data and access to stored data. The need for security in data storage has already been mentioned. The greater question has to do with whether data should be stored at all, and, if so, in what form. Some institutions have elected to destroy the original questionnaires and any computer cards or tapes as soon as the tabulation has been completed. Other institutions save the questionnaires and cards for a few weeks in case of any doubts about the accuracy of tabulation; then they destroy the original instruments and any computer cards or tapes. Still other institutions destroy the questionnaires but save the computer cards indefinitely, often with identifying information removed, sometimes with it coded, sometimes with it intact. The appropriate decision for a given institution depends on a number of factors that all have to do with legitimate need for stored data in that institution. If the data are to be used, say, for research to improve the evaluation system, a legitimate need for stored data may exist. In such cases the nature of the research and the security of the data storage facility help define the form of data storage (e.g., identifying information removed, coded, or intact.) There is a tendency on the part of some faculty, particularly before the potential importance of evaluative data is realized, to discard their reports and later to request reruns of the original reports. These reanalyses can be a considerable nuisance for the data processing unit, but they may be legitimate requests. If so, then data will need to be stored in such a fashion as to make honoring these requests feasible and economical. (This particular need diminishes as faculty come to realize the utility of these data, especially for personnel decisions, and when additional copies of reports are kept in personnel files.) Whatever policy is established, the details of that policy should be made known to all faculty in order that sometimes serious misunderstandings can be avoided.

Refining the Evaluation Program

The day-to-day involvement of experts in evaluation and measurement has already been recommended; where such experts are not readily available, consultants from other institutions should be brought in for occasional review of the system. Continuing specialist involvement is especially important in the early months and even years of an evaluation program, because early decisions form the character of the program and because wrong decisions are extremely difficult to make right. A faculty or faculty-student advisory committee is equally desirable, since these people can often raise questions and point out deficiencies that bother or confuse many users of the system. Occasional surveys of faculty and students may provide additional information of that sort. Also, faculty on instructional committees and promotion/tenure committees, as well as administrators at various levels, should be queried for their reactions to the system. All of these people look at evaluation from different perspectives, and each has a legitimate point of view to present. These joint efforts, perhaps especially the conflicts and disagreements, can be expected gradually to produce better and better faculty evaluation systems.

Appendix: Representative Student Evaluation Forms

STUDENT OPINION SURVEY

This questionnaire gives you the opportunity to share your views about certain aspects of this course with your instructor. For each item below, please indicate the response closest to your opinion by circling the appropriate number. Please circle only one number for each item.

Thank you for your help.

Course_____

Instructor_____

Quarter & Year_____

GENERAL

measurement services center
9 clarence avenue s.e. minneapolis, minnesota 55414

		Very Strongly Disagree	Strongly Disagree	Disagree	Agree	Strongly Agree	Very Strongly Agree	Most Strongly Agree
The INSTRUCTOR:								
1.	clearly presented the subject matter.	1	2	3	4	5	6	7
2.	was approachable.	1	2	3	4	5	6	7
3.	got me interested in her/his subject.	1	2	3	4	5	6	7
4.	raised challenging questions.	1	2	3	4	5	6	7
5.	when appropriate, related course material to other areas of knowledge.	1	2	3	4	5	6	7
The READING MATERIAL--including the textbook:								
6.	held my attention easily.	1	2	3	4	5	6	7
7.	was clearly written.	1	2	3	4	5	6	7
8.	served well the purpose for which it was intended.	1	2	3	4	5	6	7
The TESTS:								
9.	concentrated on the important points and topics in the subject matter.	1	2	3	4	5	6	7
10.	seemed to have been carefully and conscientiously prepared.	1	2	3	4	5	6	7
11.	were about the right length.	1	2	3	4	5	6	7
12.	were clearly worded.	1	2	3	4	5	6	7
13.	seemed to be good measures of my knowledge and understanding.	1	2	3	4	5	6	7
In GENERAL:								
14.	procedures for determining grades were appropriate for this course.	1	2	3	4	5	6	7
15.	the amount of work required was appropriate for the number of credits offered.	1	2	3	4	5	6	7
16.	adequate information about how well I was doing was readily available.	1	2	3	4	5	6	7
17.	adequate help was available when I needed it.	1	2	3	4	5	6	7
18.	my responsibilities in the course were clearly defined.	1	2	3	4	5	6	7

Please continue on the other side. ➡

19. How much did you like the SUBJECT MATTER of the course, forgetting about the instructor?

1	2	3	4	5	6	7
Disliked Intensely	Disliked Greatly	Disliked Somewhat	Liked Somewhat	Liked A Lot	Liked Very Much	Liked Exceptionally Well

20. How much did you like this instructor AS A PERSON?

1	2	3	4	5	6	7
Disliked Intensely	Disliked Considerably	Disliked Somewhat	Liked Somewhat	Liked A Lot	Liked Very Much	Liked Exceptionally Well

21. How would you rate this instructor's OVERALL TEACHING ABILITY?

1	2	3	4	5	6	7
Very Poor	Poor	Fair	Good	Very Good	Excellent	Exceptionally Good

22. How much would you say you LEARNED from this instructor?

1	2	3	4	5	6	7
Almost Nothing	Very Little	Little	A Fair Amount	Much	Very Much	An Exceptional Amount

23. How much EFFORT did you put into this course?

1	2	3	4	5	6	7
Almost None	Very Little	Little	A Fair Amount	Much	Very Much	An Exceptional Amount

24. In which YEAR in school are you?

1	2	3	4	5	6
Freshman	Sophomore	Junior	Senior	Graduate	Adult Special

25. Was this specific course REQUIRED of you?

1	2
Yes	No

26. What is your overall cumulative GRADE-POINT AVERAGE at the University of Minnesota?

1	2	3	4	5
2.0 or Below	2.1-2.5	2.6-3.0	3.1-3.5	3.6-4.0

27. Which SEX are you?

1	2
Female	Male

Your instructor may provide some additional questions. If so, please use this section to answer them. If not, please leave this section blank.

28. 1 2 3 4 5 6 7   32. 1 2 3 4 5 6 7
29. 1 2 3 4 5 6 7   33. 1 2 3 4 5 6 7
30. 1 2 3 4 5 6 7   34. 1 2 3 4 5 6 7
31. 1 2 3 4 5 6 7   35. 1 2 3 4 5 6 7

STUDENT
OPINION
SURVEY

This questionnaire gives you
an opportunity to evaluate
this course in your own words
and to offer recommendations
for its improvement. Please
be frank, specific, and constructive.

Course _____

Instructor _____

Quarter &
Year _____

SUPPLEMENT measurement services center
9 clarence avenue s.e. minneapolis, minnesota 55414

1. Please describe yourself in order to give your instructor an idea of
   your point of view:

   Major _____   GPA _____

   Year in School _____   Grading Option: A-N S-N Other

   Vocational/Educational Plans: _____

   _____

2. For what reasons did you take this course?

→

3. How much and in what ways do you feel this course has contributed to your education?

4. Please comment on the following characteristics of the instructor as they enhanced or detracted from the course:

His/her grasp of the material

Communication skills

Attitudes toward students

5. What things about this course or instructor particularly heightened or diminished your motivation really to 'get into' the subject matter?

6. Please comment briefly on the particular strengths and/or weaknesses of any or all of the following as they relate to your experience in this course or to what you got out of it:

Reading Material

Tests

Handouts

Written Assignments

Teaching Assistant(s)

Other Students

Yourself

$\longrightarrow$

7. What were the most satisfying things about the course and the instructor? The most disappointing?

8. Please make any further evaluative comments or suggestions for improvement here.

Thanks for your help.

SPECIFIC STUDENT OPINION SURVEY

READING MATERIALS

This questionnaire gives you the opportunity to share with your instructor your views about the reading materials used in this course. For each item below, please indicate the response closest to your opinion by circling the appropriate number. Please circle only one number for each item.

Thanks for your help.

Course _____

Instructor _____

Quarter & Year _____

measurement services center
9 clarence avenue s.e. minneapolis, minnesota 55414

	Very Strongly Disagree	Strongly Disagree	Disagree	Agree	Strongly Agree	Very Strongly Agree	Most Strongly Agree
1. The instructor seems to have chosen these reading materials carefully.	1	2	3	4	5	6	7
2. The instructor gave an adequate explanation of the purpose to be served by these materials.	1	2	3	4	5	6	7
3. The instructor was helpful in indicating how much attention to give to the different parts of these materials, i.e., which parts to skim, which to read carefully, which to analyze, etc.	1	2	3	4	5	6	7
4. The writing style was generally very clear.	1	2	3	4	5	6	7
5. The substance of these materials was generally of high quality.	1	2	3	4	5	6	7
6. The writing style heightened my interest in the content.	1	2	3	4	5	6	7
7. These materials held my attention easily.	1	2	3	4	5	6	7
8. I learned from these materials much that I had not known.	1	2	3	4	5	6	7
9. These materials definitely stimulated my thinking.	1	2	3	4	5	6	7
10. These materials were of appropriate difficulty for a course of this level and type--neither too complex nor too simple.	1	2	3	4	5	6	7
11. The amount of material to be read was just right for a course of this level and type.	1	2	3	4	5	6	7
12. These materials were readily available or accessible.	1	2	3	4	5	6	7
13. These materials served well the purpose for which they were intended.	1	2	3	4	5	6	7
14. These materials complemented the other parts of the course.	1	2	3	4	5	6	7
15. These materials contributed significantly to my understanding of the topics in this course.	1	2	3	4	5	6	7

Please continue on the other side. →

16. Of the reading for this course that was scheduled to have been completed by now, how much have you finished?

1	2	3	4	5
Very Little	Less Than Half	About Half	More Than Half	Almost All

17. Compared to your level of interest <u>before</u> you did this reading, did these materials increase or decrease your interest in the subject matter?

1	2	3	4	5
Decreased Much	Decreased Somewhat	Left the Same	Increased Somewhat	Increased Much

18. In which YEAR in school are you?

1	2	3	4	5	6
Freshman	Sophomore	Junior	Senior	Graduate	Adult Special

19. Was this specific course REQUIRED of you?

1	2
Yes	No

20. What is your cumulative GRADE-POINT AVERAGE at the University of Minnesota?

1	2	3	4	5
2.0 or below	2.1-2.5	2.6-3.0	3.1-3.5	3.6-4.0

21. Under which GRADING OPTION are you taking this course?

1	2	3
A-N	S-N	Other

22. Which SEX are you?

1	2
Female	Male

Your instructor may provide some additional questions. If so, please use this section to answer them. If not, please leave this section blank.

23.	1	2	3	4	5	6	7		26.	1	2	3	4	5	6	7
24.	1	2	3	4	5	6	7		27.	1	2	3	4	5	6	7
25.	1	2	3	4	5	6	7		28.	1	2	3	4	5	6	7

Please add any further evaluative comments or constructive suggestions about the reading materials.

student evaluation of instruction

part I: student evaluation form

Instructor _____

Course _____

Quarter & Year _____

ⅿ𝒮university measurement services center
9 clarence avenue s.e. minneapolis, minnesota 55414

LISTED BELOW ARE A NUMBER OF ITEMS DESCRIBING INSTRUCTOR BEHAVIOR.	FREQUENCY OF OCCURENCE	IMPORTANCE
Each item contains TWO PARTS. BOTH parts must be answered.	Indicate the frequency of occurence of each behavior by circling the number of the appropriate alternative.	Indicate the importance of this behavior to you as it relates to the course being evaluated. Circle the number of the appropriate alternative.

The Instructor:

Frequency columns: Never / Rarely / Sometimes / Usually / Always
Importance columns: Not Important / Slightly Important / Important / Very Important / Extremely Important

The Instructor:	Never	Rarely	Sometimes	Usually	Always		Not Imp.	Slightly Imp.	Important	Very Imp.	Extremely Imp.
1. Is concerned about the effectiveness of his teaching.	1	2	3	4	5	1 2	1	2	3	4	5
2. Is genuinely interested in students.	1	2	3	4	5		1	2	3	4	5
3. Is well informed on the material presented.	1	2	3	4	5	5 6	1	2	3	4	5
4. Clearly indicates what material tests will cover.	1	2	3	4	5		1	2	3	4	5
5. Stimulates curiosity about the subject matter.	1	2	3	4	5	9 10	1	2	3	4	5
6. Has an interesting style of presentation.	1	2	3	4	5		1	2	3	4	5
7. Organizes his lectures well.	1	2	3	4	5		1	2	3	4	5
8. Clearly interprets abstract ideas and theories.	1	2	3	4	5	15 16	1	2	3	4	5
9. Attempts to stimulate creative abilities.	1	2	3	4	5		1	2	3	4	5
10. Keeps the course moving rapidly enough for the material.	1	2	3	4	5	19 20	1	2	3	4	5
11. Makes good use of examples and illustrations.	1	2	3	4	5		1	2	3	4	5
12. Relates the material of this course with other areas of knowledge.	1	2	3	4	5		1	2	3	4	5
13. Presents or allows various points of view.	1	2	3	4	5	25 26	1	2	3	4	5
14. Discusses recent developments in the field.	1	2	3	4	5		1	2	3	4	5
15. Is aware when students are having difficulty in understanding a topic.	1	2	3	4	5	29 30	1	2	3	4	5
16. Makes it clear how each topic fits into the course.	1	2	3	4	5		1	2	3	4	5
17. Gives explanations which are clear and to the point.	1	2	3	4	5		1	2	3	4	5
18. Welcomes questions from students.	1	2	3	4	5	35 36	1	2	3	4	5
19. Is available for individual help.	1	2	3	4	5		1	2	3	4	5

(over)

FREQUENCY OF OCCURRENCE   IMPORTANCE

| | Never | Rarely | Sometimes | Usually | Always | | Not Important | Slightly Important | Important | Very Important | Extremely Important |

The Instructor:

20. Clearly defines student responsibilities in the course.   1 2 3 4 5 | column 39 40 | 1 2 3 4 5

21. Demands a reasonable amount of work.   1 2 3 4 5 | 1 2 3 4 5

22. Invites criticism of his own ideas.   1 2 3 4 5 | 1 2 3 4 5

23. Is enthusiastic about his subject.   1 2 3 4 5 | 45 46 | 1 2 3 4 5

24. Is humorous at appropriate times.   1 2 3 4 5 | 1 2 3 4 5

25. Gives adequate information during the course regarding student progress through quizzes, tests or other feedback.   1 2 3 4 5 | 49 50 | 1 2 3 4 5

26. Encourages class discussion.   1 2 3 4 5 | 1 2 3 4 5

Please use items 27 through 31 for responding to any items specially developed by the instructor.

27. _____   1 2 3 4 5 | 1 2 3 4 5

28. _____   1 2 3 4 5 | 55 56 | 1 2 3 4 5

29. _____   1 2 3 4 5 | 1 2 3 4 5

30. _____   1 2 3 4 5 | 59 60 | 1 2 3 4 5

31. _____   1 2 3 4 5 | 1 2 3 4 5

FOR ITEMS 32 THROUGH 38, Please circle the number of the appropriate response. Circle only one number for each item.

32. What is the overall value of this course to you?

| Not Valuable 1 | Slightly Valuable 2 | Valuable 3 | Valuable 4 | Valuable 5 |

column 63

33. Which sex are you?

1. Male   2. Female

64

34. Which of the following apply to you?

1. Freshman   3. Junior   5. Graduate Student   7. Other
2. Sophomore   4. Senior   6. Adult Special

65

35. What is your overall cumulative grade point average (GPA)?

1. 1.99 or less   3. 2.51 - 2.99   5. 3.51 - 4.00
2. 2.00 - 2.50   4. 3.00 - 3.50

66

36. What grade do you expect to get in this course?

1. A   4. D   7. N
2. B(S)   5. F(U)   8. Audit
3. C   6. P   9. Other (please specify)_____

67

37. Is this course within your major program?

1. Yes   2. No

68

38. Is this course required or optional?

1. Required   2. Optional

69

STUDENT REACTIONS TO INSTRUCTION AND COURSES -- SHORT FORM

By giving thoughtful and honest answers to these questions, you will help your instructor improve this course and his teaching procedures. Omit items which are not applicable to your instructor or this course.

PART I. *Describe your instructor's teaching procedures by using the following code:*
1 = Hardly Ever   2 = Occasionally
3 = Sometimes   4 = Frequently
*   5 = Almost Always*

The Instructor:

1. Promoted teacher-student discussion (as opposed to mere responses to questions).
2. Found ways to help students answer their own questions.
3. Encouraged students to express themselves freely and openly.
4. Seemed enthusiastic about the subject matter.
5. Changed his approach to meet new situations.
6. Spoke with expressiveness and variety in tone of voice.
7. Demonstrated the importance and significance of his subject matter.
8. Made presentations which were dry and dull.
9. Made it clear how each topic fit into the course.
10. Explained the reasons for his criticisms of students' academic performance.
11. Encouraged student comments even when they turned out to be incorrect or irrelevant.
12. Summarized material in a manner which aided retention.
13. Stimulated students to intellectual effort beyond that required by most courses.
14. Stated clearly the objectives of the course.
15. Explained course material clearly, and explanations were to the point.
16. Related course material to real life situations.
17. Gave examinations which stressed unnecessary memorization.
18. Gave examination questions which were unreasonably detailed (picky).

PART II. *On the next four questions, compare this course with others you have taken at this institution, using the following code:*
1 = Much Less than Most Courses
2 = Less than Most   3 = About Average
4 = More than Most   5 = Much More than Most

The Course:

19. Amount of reading.
20. Amount of work in other (non-reading) assignments.
21. Difficulty of subject matter.
22. Degree to which the course hung together (various topics and class activities were related to each other).

PART III. *Compare the progress you have made in this course with that made in other courses you have taken at this college or university, using the following code:*
1 = Lowest 10% of Courses I have taken here
2 = Next 20%   3 = Middle 40%
4 = Next 20%   5 = Upper 10%

Your Progress:

23. Gaining factual knowledge (terminology, classifications, methods, trends).
24. Learning fundamental principles, generalizations, or theories.
25. Learning to apply course material to improve rational thinking, problem-solving and decision making.
26. Developing specific skills, competencies and points of view needed by professionals in the field most closely related to this course.
27. Learning how professionals in this field go about the process of gaining new knowledge.
28. Developing creative capacities.
29. Developing a sense of personal responsibility (self-reliance, self-discipline).
30. Gaining a broader understanding and appreciation of intellectual-cultural activity (music, science, literature, etc.).
31. Developing skill in expressing myself orally or in writing.
32. Discovering the implications of the course material for understanding myself (interests, talents, values, etc.).

PART IV. *Describe your personal attitudes and behavior in this course, using the following code:*
1 = Definitely False   2 = More False than True
3 = Inbetween   4 = More True than False
*   5 = Definitely True*

Self-Rating:

33. I worked harder on this course than on most courses I have taken.
34. I had a strong desire to take this course.
35. I would like to take another class from this instructor.
36. As a result of taking this course, I have more positive feelings toward this field of study.

If your instructor has extra questions, answer them in the space designated on the Answer Form.

Your comments on how the instructor might improve this course or his teaching are invited; use the space provided.

COURSE EVALUATION—PRINCETON UNIVERSITY

QUESTIONNAIRE COPYRIGHT BY PRINCETON UNIVERSITY, 1971. ALL RIGHTS RESERVED.

RATINGS KEY

0 = NOT APPLICABLE
1 = UNACCEPTABLE
2 = POOR
3 = FAIR
4 = GOOD
5 = EXCELLENT

LEAVE BLANK / COURSE NO. / DEPT. NO.

LECTURES

1. Rate the general quality of lectures as a whole

Rate the quality of lectures in terms of the degree to which they:

2. Covered the material at an appropriate intellectual level—neither too complicated nor too simple
3. Clearly presented the relevant subject matter
4. Stimulated your intellectual curiosity and provoked independent thinking

READINGS

5. Rate the general quality of readings as a whole

Rate the quality of readings in terms of the degree to which they:

6. Were of the right level of difficulty—neither too complicated nor too simple
7. Clearly presented the relevant subject matter
8. Stimulated your intellectual curiosity and provoked independent thinking
9. Were coordinated with other parts of the course

PRECEPTS OR CLASSES

10. Rate the general quality of precepts or classes as a whole

Rate the quality of precepts or classes on each of the following items

11. The instructor's responsiveness to students' concerns and questions
12. The instructor's ability to encourage broad student participation
13. The instructor's ability to help clarify readings and lectures
14. The instructor's ability to raise challenging questions

PAPERS, REPORTS AND PROBLEM SETS

Rate each of the following aspects of papers, reports, problem sets and other exercises in this course

15. The overall value of the papers, reports, problem sets and other exercises to this course
16. The helpfulness of the instructor's comments in response to your written work
17. The quality of guidance given by the instructor in choice of topics and suggestions for relevant research

LABORATORIES

18. Rate the quality of laboratories as a whole

Rate the quality of laboratories in terms of the degree to which they:

19. Were useful to you as a supplement to the lectures and readings—added significantly to the course
20. Contained the right amount of structure and guidance by the instructor

SEMINARS

21. Rate the quality of seminars as a whole

Rate the quality of seminars on each of the following items:

22. The degree to which you felt part of a continuing scholarly discussion
23. The degree to which you felt a sense of challenge, insight and discovery
24. The instructor's ability to conduct discussions
25. The instructor's ability to encourage broad student participation
26. The instructor's ability to raise stimulating, provocative questions

LANGUAGE COURSES

Rate the quality of language instruction in terms of the degree to which you found that it:

27. Helped you to read the language
28. Helped you to understand the language
29. Helped you to speak the language
30. Helped you to write the language

Rate the utility of each of the following in assisting you to master the language

31. Classes
32. Drills
33. Textbooks
34. Tests
35. Laboratories
36. Rate the general quality of the course as a whole

OVERALL RATINGS

37. How would you rate the overall quality of teaching in this course?

In relation to your objectives in this course and compared to other courses you have taken at Princeton, how would your rate it in terms of its contribution to each of the following:

38. Your capacity for critical evaluation of the subject matter
39. Your increased interest in the field
40. Rate the overall effectiveness of quizzes or examinations in this course as educational devices
41. Overall, how well integrated were the various parts of this course?

CLASS INSTRUCTOR / DRILL OR LAB INSTRUCTOR / LECTURER / PRECEPTOR

Educational Testing Service. Princeton, N. J. 08540

INSTRUCTIONS ON REVERSE SIDE

698B82P36D

INSTRUCTOR AND COURSE APPRAISAL

INSTRUCTOR'S NAME   COURSE TITLE AND NUMBER   DATE

PLEASE RESPOND TO ANY ITEMS IN THIS SECTION BY MARKING THE APPROPRIATE SPACES.
USE PENCIL ONLY. ERASE CHANGES OR CORRECTIONS COMPLETELY.

CLASS	SEX	GRADE YOU EXPECT	MAJOR AREA	MAJOR AREA CON'T
FRESHMAN	FEMALE			
SOPHOMORE	MALE	PASS/A	EDUCATION	SCIENCE
JUNIOR		B	HUMANITIES	TECHNOLOGY
SENIOR		C	LAW	OTHER
GRAD		D	MEDICINE	
OTHER		FAIL/F	PHARMACY	

PLEASE READ EACH STATEMENT CAREFULLY, THEN SELECT ONE OF THESE FIVE ALTERNATIVES:
STRONGLY AGREE (SA), AGREE (A), UNDECIDED (U), DISAGREE (D), STRONGLY DISAGREE (SD).

I UNDERSTAND EASILY WHAT MY INSTRUCTOR IS SAYING.
DIFFICULT TOPICS ARE STRUCTURED IN EASILY UNDERSTOOD WAYS.
MY INSTRUCTOR SPEAKS AUDIBLY AND CLEARLY.
THIS COURSE SUPPLIES ME WITH AN EFFECTIVE RANGE OF CHALLENGES.
IN THIS COURSE, I ALWAYS FELT CHALLENGED AND MOTIVATED TO LEARN.
THIS COURSE MOTIVATES ME TO TAKE ADDITIONAL RELATED COURSES.
THIS COURSE FOSTERS RESPECT FOR NEW POINTS OF VIEW.
THIS COURSE HAS EFFECTIVELY CHALLENGED ME TO THINK.
RELATIONSHIPS AMONG COURSE TOPICS ARE CLEARLY EXPLAINED.
THIS COURSE BUILDS UNDERSTANDING OF CONCEPTS AND PRINCIPLES.
MY INSTRUCTOR EVALUATES OFTEN AND PROVIDES HELP WHERE NEEDED.
MY INSTRUCTOR APPEARS TO GRASP QUICKLY WHAT A STUDENT IS SAYING.
MY INSTRUCTOR IS CAREFUL AND PRECISE WHEN ANSWERING QUESTIONS.
THIS COURSE SHOWS A SENSITIVITY TO INDIVIDUAL INTERESTS/ABILITIES.
STUDENTS PROCEED AT THEIR OWN PACE IN THIS COURSE.
EACH STUDENT IS ENCOURAGED TO CONTRIBUTE TO CLASS LEARNING.
I FEEL THAT I AM AN IMPORTANT MEMBER OF THIS CLASS.
I AM FREE TO EXPRESS AND EXPLAIN MY OWN VIEWS IN CLASS.
MY INSTRUCTOR DEALS FAIRLY AND IMPARTIALLY WITH ME.
THE CLIMATE OF THIS CLASS IS CONDUCIVE TO LEARNING.
THE OBJECTIVES OF THIS COURSE WERE CLEARLY EXPLAINED TO ME.
I WAS ABLE TO SET AND ACHIEVE SOME OF MY OWN GOALS.
THE COURSE CONTENT IS CONSISTENT WITH MY PRIOR EXPECTATIONS.
COURSE OBJECTIVES ALLOW ME TO KNOW WHEN I AM MAKING PROGRESS.
THIS COURSE INCLUDES ADEQUATE INFORMATION ON CAREER OPPORTUNITIES.
THE RELATIONSHIP OF THIS COURSE TO MY EDUCATION IS APPARENT.
ONE REAL STRENGTH OF THIS COURSE IS THE CLASSROOM DISCUSSION.
MY INSTRUCTOR DEVELOPS CLASSROOM DISCUSSION SKILLFULLY.
MY FINAL GRADE WILL ACCURATELY REFLECT MY OVERALL PERFORMANCE.
MY INSTRUCTOR HAS A REALISTIC DEFINITION OF GOOD PERFORMANCE.
COURSE TOPICS ARE DEALT WITH IN SUFFICIENT DEPTH.
I PUT A GOOD DEAL OF EFFORT INTO THIS COURSE.
I FIND THE COURSE EMPHASIS ON INDIVIDUAL PROJECTS STIMULATING.
I AM SATISFIED WITH MY ACCOMPLISHMENTS IN THIS COURSE.
THESE ITEMS LET ME APPRAISE THIS COURSE FULLY AND FAIRLY.
MY INSTRUCTOR MOTIVATES ME TO DO MY BEST WORK.
MY INSTRUCTOR EXPLAINS DIFFICULT TOPICS AND MATERIAL CLEARLY.
COURSE ASSIGNMENTS ARE INTERESTING AND STIMULATING.
OVERALL, THIS COURSE IS AMONG THE BEST I HAVE TAKEN.
OVERALL, THIS INSTRUCTOR IS AMONG THE BEST TEACHERS I HAVE KNOWN.

ON ANOTHER SHEET, DESCRIBE WHAT YOU LIKED BEST ABOUT THIS COURSE.
ON ANOTHER SHEET, DESCRIBE WHAT YOU LIKED LEAST ABOUT THIS COURSE.
WHAT IMPROVEMENTS WOULD YOU RECOMMEND FOR THIS COURSE?

(Each statement is followed by response options: SA A U D SD)

Primary Bibliography

Aleamoni, L. M., and Spencer, R. E. 1973. The Illinois Course Evaluation Questionnaire: A description of its development and a report of some of its results. *Educational and Psychological Measurement, 33(3)*, 669–84.

Aleamoni, L. M., and Yimer, M. 1973. An investigation of the relationship between colleague rating, student rating, research productivity, and academic rank in rating instructional effectiveness. *Journal of Educational Psychology, 64,* 274–277.

Aleamoni, L. M. 1974. The usefulness of student evaluations in improving college teaching. Urbana: Measurement and Research Division, Office of Instructional Resources, University of Illinois.

Anikeeff, A. M. 1953. Factors affecting student evaluation of college faculty members. *Journal of Applied Psychology, 37,* 458–460.

Asher, E. J., Jr. 1969. Differential weighting of teacher evaluation criteria. Paper presented at the meeting of the Association for Institutional Research, Chicago, May.

Astin, A. W., and Holland, J. L., 1961. The Environmental Assessment Technique: A way to measure college environments. *Journal of Educational Psychology, 52,* 308–16.

Astin, A. W., Comstock, C., Epperson, D. C., Greeley, A. M., Katz, J., and Kauffman, J. F. 1974. *Faculty development in a time of retrenchment.* New Rochelle (N.Y.): The Group for Human Development in Higher Education and *Change* Magazine.

Baier, D. E. 1952. Reply to Travers's "A critical review of the validity and rationale of the forced-choice technique." *Psychological Bulletin, 48,* 421–434.

Barnette, W. L., Jr., ed. 1968. *Readings in Psychological Tests and Measurements.* Homewood, Ill.: Dorsey Press.

Bass, B. M., Cascio, W. F., and O'Connor, E. J. 1974. Magnitude of expressions of frequency and amount. *Journal of Applied Psychology, 59(3),* 313–20.

Bejar, I. I., and Doyle, K. O., Jr. 1974*a*. The effect of prior expectation on the structure and elevation of student ratings of teaching behavior. Minneapolis: Measurement Services Center, University of Minnesota.

Bejar, I. I., and Doyle, K. O., Jr. 1974*b*. Expectations, First Impressions, and Evaluations. Minneapolis: Measurement Services Center, University of Minnesota.

Bejar, I. I., and Doyle, K. O., Jr. 1974c. Generalizability of factor structures underlying student ratings of instruction. American Educational Research Association Convention, Chicago.

Bendig, A. W. 1952. Statistical report on a revision of the Miami instructor rating sheet. *Journal of Educational Psychology, 43,* 423–29.

Bendig, A. W. 1953. Student achievement in introductory psychology and student ratings of the competence and empathy of their instructors. *Journal of Psychology, 36,* 427–433.

Bendig, A. W. 1954. A factor analysis of student ratings of psychology instructors on the Purdue Scale. *Journal of Educational Psychology, 45,* 385–393.

Berdie, D. R., and Anderson, J. F. 1974. *Questionnaires: Design and Use.* Metuchen (N.J.): Scarecrow Press.

Berkshire, J. R., and Highland, R. W. 1953. Forced-choice performance ratings—A methodological study. *Personnel Psychology, 6,* 356–78.

Betz, E. L., Klingensmith, J. E., and Menne, J. W. 1970. The measurement and analysis of college student satisfaction. *Measurement and Evaluation in Guidance, 3,* 110–18.

Blackburn, R. T., and Clark, M. 1971. An assessment of faculty performance: Some correlates between administrator, colleague, student, and self ratings. Ann Arbor: Center for the Study of Higher Education, University of Michigan. Mimeographed.

Bloom, B. S., ed. 1956. *Taxonomy of educational objectives: The classification of educational goals. Handbook 1. Cognitive domain.* New York: McKaye.

Bloom, B. S., Hastings, J. T., and Madaus, G. F., eds. 1971. *Handbook on the Formative and Summative Evaluation of Student Learning.* New York: McGraw-Hill.

Blum, M. M. 1936. An investigation of the relation existing between students' grades and their ratings of an instructor's ability to teach. *Journal of Educational Psychology, 27,* 217–221.

Boardman, C. W. 1928. Professional tests as measures of teaching efficiency in high school. *Teachers' College Contributions to Education,* Number 327.

Borman, W. C., and Vallon, W. R. 1974. A view of what can happen when behavioral expectation scales are developed in one setting and used in another. *Journal of Applied Psychology, 59(2),* 197–201.

Bowman, E. C. 1934. Pupil ratings of student teachers. *Educational Administration and Supervision, 20,* 141–46.

Brookover, W. B. 1940. Person-person interaction between teachers and pupils and teaching effectiveness. *Journal of Educational Research, 34,* 272–87.

Bryan, R. C. 1937. Pupil rating of secondary school teachers. *Teachers' College Contributions to Education,* Number 708.

Burnaska, R. F., and Hollmann, T. D. 1974. An empirical comparison of the relative effects of rater response biases on three rating scale formats. *Journal of Applied Psychology, 59(3)* 307–12.

Caffrey, B. 1969. Lack of bias in student evaluations of teachers. Proceedings of the 77th Annual Convention of the American Psychological Association, *4,* 641–642.

Campbell, J. P., Dunnette, M. D., Arvey, R. D., and Hellervik, L. V. 1973. The development and evaluation of behaviorally based rating scales. *Journal of Applied Psychology, 57,* 15–22.

Cattell, R. B. 1964. Validity and reliability: A proposed more basic set of concepts. *Journal of Educational Psychology, 55,* 1–22.

Centra, J. A. 1972. Two studies on the utility of student ratings for improving teaching. SIR Report No. 2. Princeton, N.J.: Educational Testing Service.

Centra, J. A. 1973*a*. Self-ratings of college teachers: A comparison with student ratings. *Journal of Educational Measurement, 10,* 287–295.

Centra, J. A. 1973*b*. The relationship between student and alumni ratings of teachers. Research Bulletin 73–39. Princeton, N.J.: Educational Testing Service.

Centra, J. 1974. College teaching: Who should evaluate it? *Findings, 1(1).* Princeton (N.J.): Educational Testing Service.

Coffman, W. E. 1954. Determining students' concepts of effective teaching from their ratings of instructors. *Journal of Educational Psychology, 45,* 277–286.

Cohen, J., and Humphreys, L. G. 1960. Memorandum to faculty. University of Illinois, Department of Psychology. Mimeographed.

Cosgrove, D. S. 1959. Diagnostic rating of teacher performance. *Journal of Educational Psychology, 50,* 200–204.

Costin, F. 1966. Intercorrelations between students' and course chairmen's ratings of instructors. University of Illinois, Division of General Studies. Mimeographed.

Costin, F. 1968. *Survey of opinions about lecturers.* University of Illinois, Department of Psychology. Mimeographed.

Costin, F., Greenough, W. T., and Menges, R. J. 1971. Student ratings of college teaching: Reliability, validity, and usefulness. *Review of Educational Research, 41,* 511–535.

Crannell, C. W. 1953. A preliminary attempt to identify the factors in student-instructor evaluation. *Journal of Psychology, 36,* 417–422.

Crittenden, K. S., and Norr, J. L. 1974. Student values and teacher evaluation: A problem in person perception. *Sociometry, 36,* 143–51.

Cronbach, L. J. 1951. Coefficient alpha and the internal structure of tests. *Psychometrika, 16,* 297–334.

Davenport, K. 1944. An investigation into pupil rating of certain teaching practices. *Purdue University Studies in Higher Education,* Number 49.

Dawis, R. V., Lofquist, L. H., and Weiss, D. J. 1968. *A Theory of Work Adjustment (A Revision).* Minnesota Studies in Vocational Rehabilitation, 23. Minneapolis: Work Adjustment Project, University of Minnesota.

Derry, J. O., and the Staff of the Measurement and Research Center. 1974. The Cafeteria System: A new approach to course and instructor evaluation. Institutional Research Bulletin 74–1, Measurement and Research Center, Purdue University, Lafayette, Indiana.

Deshpande, A. S., Webb, S. C., and Marks, E. 1970. Student perceptions of engineering instructor behaviors and their relationships to the evaluation of instructors and courses. *American Educational Research Journal, 7,* 289–305.

Detchen, L. 1940. Shall the student rate the professor? *Journal of Higher Education, 11,* 146–54.

de Wolf, V. A. 1974. Student ratings of instruction in post secondary institutions: A comprehensive annotated bibliography of research reported since 1968. Volume I. Seattle: University of Washington, Bureau of Testing.

Doyle, K. O., Jr. 1972. Construction and evaluation of scales for rating college instructors. Unpublished PhD thesis, University of Minnesota. *Dissertation Abstracts International,* 1972, *33(5–A),* 2163. (Ann Arbor, Michigan: University Microfilms. (Order No. 72–27, 746)

Doyle, K. O., Jr., and Bejar, I. I. 1973. Computer-generated narrative-format instructor-assistance classroom-data reports. American Educational Research Association Convention, New Orleans.

Doyle, K. O., Jr., Bejar, I. I., and Whitely, S. E. 1974. Norms for the Student Opinion Survey. Minneapolis: Measurement Services Center, University of Minnesota.

Doyle, K. O., Jr., and Whitely, S. E. 1972. Student evaluations revisited: A reply to Rodin and Rodin. Minneapolis: Measurement Services Center, University of Minnesota.

Doyle, K. O., Jr., and Whitely, S. E. 1974. Student ratings as criteria for effective teaching. *American Educational Research Journal, 11(3),* 259–74.

Drucker, A. J., and Remmers, H. H. 1951. Do alumni and students differ in their attitudes toward instructors? *Journal of Educational Psychology, 42,* 129–143.

Dunnette, M. D. 1966. *Personnel Selection and Placement,* Belmont, Cal.: Wadsworth.

Echandia, P. P. 1964. A methodological study and factor analytic validation of forced-choice performance ratings of college instructors. *Dissertation Abstracts, 25(4),* 2605–2606.

Eckert, R. E. 1950. Ways of evaluating college teaching. *School and Society, 71,* 65–69.

Eckert, R. E. and Keller, R. J., eds. 1954. *A university looks at its program: Report of the University of Minnesota Bureau of Institutional Research, 1942–52.* Minneapolis: University of Minnesota Press.

Elliott, D. H. 1950. Characteristics and relationships of various criteria of college and university teaching. *Purdue University Studies in Higher Education, 70,* 5–61.

Freedman, M. ed. 1973. Facilitating faculty development. *New Directions for Higher Education, 1* (1).

Frey, P. W. 1973. Student ratings of teaching: Validity of several rating factors. *Science, 182,* 83–85.

Gage, N. L. 1958. Ends and means in appraising college training. Conference on Appraisal of Teaching in Large Universities. University of Michigan, Ann Arbor. Mimeographed.

Gage, N. I. 1961. The appraisal of college teaching. *Journal of Higher Education, 32,* 17–22.

Gagne, F., and Allaire, D. 1974. Summary of research data on the reliability and validity of a measure of dissatisfaction derived from Reality-Desires discrepancies. Quebec: Institute National de la Recherche Scientifique, Universite du Quebec.

Garverick, C. M., and Carter, H. D. 1962. Instructor ratings and expected grades. *California Journal of Educational Research, 13,* 218–221.

Gay, E. G., Weiss, D. J., Hendel, D. D., Dawis, R. V., and Lofquist, L. H. 1971. Manual for the Minnesota Importance Questionnaire. *Minnesota Studies in Vocational Rehabilitation,* 28. Minneapolis: Work Adjustment Project, University of Minnesota.

Gibb, C. A. 1955. Classroom behavior of the college teacher. *Educational and Psychological Measurement, 15,* 254–263.

Glass, D. C., ed. 1967. *Neurophysiology and Emotion.* New York: Rockefeller University Press and Russell Sage Foundation.

Goodhartz, A. S. 1948. Student attitudes and opinions relating to teaching at Brooklyn College. *School and Society, 68,* 345–49.

Greene, H. W., 1933. A comparison of student ratings, administrative ratings, ratings by colleagues, and relative salaries as criteria for teaching excellence. West Virginia State College Bulletin, Number 5.

Guilford, J. P. 1954. *Psychometric Methods.* New York: McGraw-Hill.

Guilford, J. P. 1967. *The Nature of Human Intelligence.* New York: McGraw-Hill.

Guilford, J. P. 1968. Intelligence, creativity, and their educational implications. San Diego: Knapp.

Guilford, J. P., and Hoepfner, R. 1966. Structure of intellect factors and their tests. *Reports of the University of Southern California,* Number 36. Los Angeles.

Guthrie, E. R. 1927. Measuring student opinion of teachers. *School and Society, 25,* 175–176.

Guthrie, E. R. 1949. The evaluation of teaching. *Educational Record, 30,* 109–115.

Guthrie, E. R. 1954. *The evaluation of teaching: A progress report.* Seattle: University of Washington. Lithoprint.

Harris, C. W., ed. 1963. *Problems in measuring change,* Madison: University of Wisconsin Press.

Heilman, J. K., and Armentrout, W. D. 1936. Rating of college teachers on ten traits by their students. *Journal of Educational Psychology, 27,* 197–216.

Henrikson, E. H. 1949. Some relations between personality, speech characteristics, and teaching effectiveness of college teachers. *Speech Monograph, 16,* 221–26.

Hildebrand, M., Wilson, R. C., and Dienst, E. R. 1971. *Evaluating university teaching.* Berkeley: Center for Research and Development in Higher Education, University of California, Berkeley.

Holmes, D. S. 1972. Effects of grades and disconfirmed grade expectancies on students' evaluations of their instructor. *Journal of Educational Psychology, 63,* 130–133.

Horst, A. P. 1949. A generalized expression for the reliability of measures. *Psychometrika, 14,* 21–32.

Hoyt, C. 1941. Test reliability obtained by analysis of variance. *Psychometrika, 6,* 153–60.

Hoyt, D. P. 1973. Measurement of instructional effectiveness. *Research in Higher Education, 1,* 367–78.

Hudelson, E. 1951. The validity of student rating of instructors. *School and Society, 73,* 265–266.

Isaacson, R. L., McKeachie, W. J., Milholland, J. E., Lin, Y. G., Hofeller, M., Baerwaldt, J. W., and Zinn, K. L. 1964. Dimensions of student evaluations of teaching. *Journal of Educational Psychology, 55*(6), 344–351.

Jackson, D. N., and Messick, S. 1967. *Problems in Human Assessment.* New York: McGraw-Hill.

Kates, R. W., and Wohlwill, J. F. 1966. Man's response to the physical environment. *Journal of Social Issues, 22(4).*

Kent, L. 1966. Student evaluation of teaching. *Educational Record, 47(3),* 376–406.

Kiresuk, T. J., and Sherman, R. E. 1968. Goal Attainment Scaling: A general method for evaluating comprehensive community mental health programs. *Community Mental Health Journal, 4(6),* 443–53.

Knight, F. B., 1922. Qualities related to success in teaching. Teachers' College Contributions to Education, Number 120.

Kohlan, R. G. 1973. A comparison of faculty evaluations early and late in the course. *The Journal of Higher Education, 44,* 587–595.

Kooker, E. W. 1968. The relationship of known college grades to course ratings on student selected items. The Journal of Psychology, *69,* 209–215.

Krathwohl, D. R., Bloom, B. S., and Masia, B. B. 1964. *Taxonomy of educational objectives: The classification of educational goals. Handbook 2. Affective domain.* New York: McKay.

Kratz, H. E. 1896. Characteristics of the best teacher as recognized by children. *Pedagogical Seminar, 3,* 413–418.

Krous, G. T. 1934. A study of traits and qualities of teachers and their effectiveness in teaching, based upon the estimates of their students. Unpublished PhD thesis, Stanford University.

Kuder, G. F., and Richardson, M. W. 1937. The theory of the estimation of test reliability. *Psychometrika, 2,* 151–160.

Levinthal, C. F., Lansky, L. M., and Andrews, O. E. 1971. Student evaluations of teacher behaviors as estimations of real-ideal descrepancies: A critique of teacher rating methods. *Journal of Educational Psychology, 62,* 104–109.

Linn, R. L., Centra, J. A., and Tucker, L. 1974. Between, within, and total group factor analyses of student ratings of instruction. Research Bulletin 74–39. Princeton (N.J.): Educational Testing Service.

Lovell, G. D., and Haner, C. F. 1955. Forced-choice scales applied to college faculty rating. *Educational and Psychological Measurement, 15,* 291–304.

McKeachie, W. J. 1969. *Teaching tips: A guidebook for the beginning college teacher.* (6th Edition) Lexington, Mass.: D. C. Heath and Company.

McKeachie, W. J. 1974. Current findings on the reliability and validity of student evaluations of teaching. University of Manitoba Symposium on College Teaching and Its Evaluation, Winnipeg.

MacKenzie, N., Eraut, M., and Jomes, H. C. 1970. *Teaching and Learning: An Introduction to new methods and resources in higher education.* UNESCO and the International Association of Universities.

McKeachie, W. J., Isaacson, R., and Milholland, J. 1964. *Research on the characteristics of effective college teaching.* Final report Cooperative Research Project No. OE 850, Office of Education, Department of Health, Education, and Welfare. Ann Arbor.

McKeachie, W. J., Lin, Y., and Mann, W. 1971. Student ratings of teacher effectiveness: Validity studies. *American Educational Research Journal, 8,* 435–445.

McKeachie, W. J., and Solomon, D. 1958. Student ratings of instructors: A validity study. *Journal of Educational Research, 51,* 379–382.

Maslow, A. H., and Zimmerman, W. 1956. College teaching ability, scholarly activity and personality. *Journal of Educational Psychology, 47,* 185–189.

Meehl, P. E. 1941. Student rating of college teachers. Unpublished Summa cum Laude Thesis, University of Minnesota.

Miller, M. T. 1971. Instructor attitudes toward, and their use of, student ratings of teacher. *Journal of Educational Psychology, 62,* 235–239.

Morsh, J. E. 1955. The Q-sort Technique as a group measure. *Educational and Psychological Measurement, 15,* 390–95.

Morsh, J. E., and Wilder, E. W. 1954. Identifying the effective instructor: A review of quantitative studies, 1900–1952, AFPTRC Research Bulletin, Air Force Personnel and Training Research Center, Lackland AFB, San Antonio, Texas.

Murray, H. A. 1938. *Explorations in personality.* New York: Oxford University Press.

Newcomb, T. 1931. An experiment designed to test the validity of a rating technique. *Journal of Educational Psychology, 22,* 279–89.

Nunnally, J. C. 1967. *Psychometric theory.* New York: McGraw-Hill.

Ostin, A. W., and Holland, J. L. 1961. The Environmental Assessment Technique: A way to measure college environments. *Journal of Educational Psychology, 52,* 308–16.

Pace, C. R. 1963. *Technical manual, College and University Environment Scales.* Princeton, N.J.: Educational Testing Service.

Parent, E. R., Vaughan, C. E., and Wharton, K. 1971. A new approach to course evaluation. *Journal of Higher Education, 42* (2), 133–38.

Patton, R. M., and Meyer, P. R. 1955. A forced-choice rating form for college teachers. *Journal of Educational Psychology, 46,* 499–503.

Rayder, N. F. 1968. College student ratings of instructors. *The Journal of Experimental Education, 37(2)*, 76–81.

Remmers, H. H. 1928. The relationship between students' marks and students' attitudes toward instructors. *School and Society, 28,* 759–760.

Remmers, H. H. 1929. The college professor as the student sees him. *Purdue University Studies in Higher Education, 11,* 5–63.

Remmers, H. H. 1930. To what extent do grades influence student ratings of instructors? *Journal of Educational Research, 21,* 314–316.

Remmers, H. H. 1939. Appraisal of college teaching through ratings and student opinion. In 27th Yearbook of the National Society of College Teachers of Education. Chicago: University of Chicago Press.

Remmers, H. H. 1960. Manual of instruction for the Purdue Rating Scale for Instructors. (Rev. ed.) West Lafayette, Ind.: University Book Store.

Remmers, H. H., and Brandenburg, G. C. 1927. Experimental data on the Purdue Rating Scale for Instructors. *Educational Administration and Supervision, 13,* 519–527.

Remmers, H. H., Martin, F. D., and Elliott, D. N. 1949. Are students' ratings of instructors related to their grades? *Purdue University Studies in Higher Education, 66,* 17–26.

Remmers, H. H., and Weisbrodt, J. A. 1965. Manual of Instructions for the Purdue Rating Scale for Instruction. (Rev. ed.) West Lafayette (Ind.): University Book Store, Purdue University.

Rodin, M. J. 1973. Can students evaluate good teaching? *Change,* Summer, 66–67, 80.

Rodin, M., and Rodin, B. 1972. Student evaluations of teachers. *Science, 177,* 1164–1166.

Root, A. R. 1931. Student ratings of teachers. *Journal of Higher Education, 2,* 311–315.

Rubenstein, J., and Mitchell, H. 1970. Feeling free, student involvement, and appreciation. *Proceedings of the 78th Annual Convention of the APA,* 623–624.

Russell, H. E. 1951. Interrelations of some indices of instructor effectiveness. Unpublished doctoral dissertation, University of Pittsburgh.

Russell, H. E., and Bendig, A. W. 1953. Investigation of the relations of student ratings of psychology instructors to their course achievement when academic aptitude is controlled. *Educational and Psychological Measurement, 13,* 626–635.

Schneider, D. J. 1973. Implicit personality theory: A review. *Psychological Bulletin, 79,* 294–309.

Sharon, A. T. 1970. Eliminating bias from student ratings of college instructors. *Journal of Applied Psychology, 54,* 278–81.

Sharon, A. T., and Bartlett, C. J. 1969. Effect of instructional conditions in producing leniency on two types of rating scales. *Personnel Psychology, 22,* 251–263.

Smeltzer, C. H., and Harter, R. S. 1934. Comparison of anonymous and signed ratings of teachers. *Educational Outlook, 8,* 76–84.

Smith, P. C., and Kendall, J. G. 1963. Retranslation of expectations: An approach to the construction of unambiguous anchoring of rating scales. *Journal of Applied Psychology, 47,* 149–55.

Sockloff, A. L., ed. 1973. *Proceedings: The first invitational conference on faculty effectiveness as evaluated by students.* Philadelphia, Pa.: Measurement and Research Center, Temple University.

Solomon, D. 1966. Teacher behavior dimensions, course characteristics, and student evaluations of teachers. *American Educational Research Journal, 3,* 36–47.

Spencer, R. E. 1968. *The Illinois course evaluation questionnaire: Manual of interpretation.* (Rev. ed.) Research report No. 270. Champaign, Ill.: University of Illinois, Office of Instructional Resources, Measurement and Research Division. Mimeographed.

Staraak, J. A. 1934. Student rating of instruction. *Journal of Higher Education, 5,* 88–90.

Starry, A. R., Derry, V. O., and Wright, G. L. 1973. An automated instructor and course appraisal system. *Educational Technology, 1973, 13,* 61–64.

Stern, G. G. 1963. *Activities Index and College Characteristics Index: scoring instructors and college norms.* Syracuse: Psychological Research Center.

Stewart, C. T., and Malpass, L. F. 1966. Estimates of achievement and ratings of instructors. *Journal of Educational Research, 59,* 347–350.

Stockford, L., and Bissell, H. W. 1949. Factors involved in establishing a merit rating scale. *Personnel, 26,* 94–118.

Taylor, E. K., and Wherry, R. W. 1951. A study of leniency in two rating systems. *Personnel Psychology, 4,* 39–47.

Travers, R. M. W. 1951. A critical review of the validity and rationale of the forced-choice technique. *Psychological Bulletin, 48,* 62–70.

Treffinger, D. J., and Feldhusen, J. F. 1970. Predicting students' ratings of instruction. *Proceedings, 78th Annual Convention, APA,* 621–622.

Voeks, V., and French, G. M. 1960. Are student ratings of teachers affected by grades? *Journal of Higher Education, 31,* 330–334.

Wahlberg, H. J., ed. 1974. *Evaluating Educational Performance.* Berkeley, Cal.: McCutchan.

Walker, B. D. 1969. An investigation of selected variables relative to the manner in which a population of junior college students evaluate their teachers. *Dissertation Abstracts, 29* (9–B), 3474.

Weaver, C. H. 1960. Instructor rating by college students. *Journal of Educational Psychology, 51,* 21–25.

Webb, W. B., and Nolan, C. Y. 1955. Student, supervisor, and self-ratings of instructional proficiency. *Journal of Educational Psychology, 46,* 42–46.

Werdell, P. R. 1967. *Course and teacher evaluation.* (2nd Ed.) Washington, D. C.: United States National Student Association.

Wherry, R. J. 1952. Control of bias in ratings. Department of the Army, The Adjutant General's Office, Personnel Research and Procedures Division, Personnel Research Branch. PRS Reports 914, 915, 919, 920, and 921.

Whitely, S. E. 1974. On the invalidity of construct validity for student ratings. Minneapolis: Measurement Services Center, University of Minnesota.

Whitely, S. E., and Doyle, K. O., Jr. 1974a. Implicit theories in student ratings of instruction. Minneapolis: Measurement Services Center, University of Minnesota.

Whitely, S. E., and Doyle, K. O., Jr. 1974b. Validity and generalizability of between-class and within-class student ratings. Minneapolis: Measurement Services Center, University of Minnesota.

Whitely, S. E., Doyle, K. O., Jr., and Hopkinson, K. 1973. Student ratings and criteria for effective teaching. Minneapolis, Minnesota: Measurement Services Center, University of Minnesota.

Supplemental Bibliography

Adams, H. L. Favorable student evaluations as a function of instructor's age. *Improving College and University Teaching,* 1973, *21,* 72.

Aleamoni, L. M. (Chair), Course and instructor evaluation. Symposium presented at the National Council on Measurement in Education Convention, Chicago, April 1972.

Aleamoni, L. M. Illinois Course Evaluation Questionnaire (CEQ) results interpretation manual Form 66 and Form 32. Research Report #331. Urbana, Illinois: Measurement and Research Division, Office of Instructional Resources, University of Illinois, 1972.

Aleamoni, L. M. A review of recent reliability and validity studies on the Illinois Course Evaluation Questionnaire (CEQ). Research Memorandum #127. Urbana, Illinois: Measurement and Research Division, Office of Instructional Resources, University of Illinois, 1972.

Aleamoni, L. M., Yimer, M., and Mahan, J. M. Teacher folklore and sensitivity of a course evaluation questionnaire. *Psychological Reports,* 1972, *31,* 607–614.

Amatora, S. M. A diagnostic teacher rating scale. *Journal of Psychology,* 1950, *30,* 395–399.

American Association of Junior Colleges. A Report to the Commission on Instruction of the American Association of Junior Colleges. Washington, D. C., 1970.

American Psychological Association. Standards for Educational and Psychological Tests and Manuals, Washington, D.C., 1966.

Apt, M. H., and Fahey, G. L. A measurement of college instructor behavior. *Scientia Paedagogica Experimentalis,* 1968, *5,* 32–39.

Armentrout, W. D. Improving college teaching by consulting the consumers. *School Executive Magazine,* 1932, *51,* 476–477.

Astin, A. W., and Lee, C. B. T. Current practices in the evaluation and training of college teachers. *Educational Record,* 1966, *47,* 361–375.

Bausell, R. B., and Magoon, J. Expected grade in a course, grade point average, and student ratings of the course and the instructor. *Educational and Psychological Measurement,* 1972, *32,* 1013–1023.

Bausell, R. B., and Magoon, J. Instructional methods and college student ratings of courses and instructors. *The Journal of Experimental Education,* 1972, *40(4),* 29–33.

Bendig, A. W. A preliminary study of the effect of academic level, sex, and course variables on student rating of psychology instructors. *Journal of Psychology,* 1952, *34,* 21–26.

Bendig, A. W. An inverted factor analysis study of student-rated introductory psychology instructors. *Journal of Experimental Education,* 1953, *21,* 333–336.

Bendig, A. W. The use of student-rating scales in the evaluation of instructors in introductory psychology. *Journal of Educational Psychology,* 1952, *43,* 167–175.

Bendig, A. W. Relation of level of course achievement of students, instructor and course ratings in introductory psychology. *Educational and Psychological Measurement,* 1953, *13,* 437–488.

Bendig, A. W. Ability and personality characteristics of introductory psychology instructors rated competent and empathetic by the students. *Journal of Educational Research,* 1955, *48,* 705–709.

Berger, W. G., and Cohen, S. H. An empirical model for the formative generalization of a student instructional rating instrument and its relation to various concepts of validity. Ann Arbor: Highway Safety Research Institute, The University of Michigan, no date.

Bills, S. C. The University Evening School of the University of Tennessee: Faculty opinions and teaching performance. *Dissertation Abstracts,* 1968, *28*(10–A), 3961–3962.

Bittner, J. R. Student evaluation of instructors' communication effectiveness. *College Student Survey,* 1968, *2,* 38–40.

Black, S. Interactions between teaching and research. *Universities Quarterly,* 1972, *26,* 348–352.

Blackburn, R. T. Letter on "Research, teaching, and faculty fate." *Science,* 1971, *172,* 1082.

Blai, B., Jr. Faculty effectiveness—a 'pilot' study of student evaluation at Harcum Junior College. Report No. IRR 71–37. Bryn Mawr, Pa.: Office of Research, Harcum Junior College, no date.

Boardman, C. W. An analysis of pupil ratings of high school teachers. *Educational Administration and Supervision,* 1930, *16,* 440–446.

Bogardus, E. S. Behavior patterns of college teachers, *Sociology and Social Research,* 1946, *30,* 484–499.

Borgatta, E. F. Student ratings of faculty, *AAUP Bulletin,* 1970, *56,* 6–7.

Borland, D. T. A comparative study of instructor ratings by students admitted to a "Disadvantaged Student" Program. *Journal of Negro Education,* 1973, *42,* 187–190.

Bousefield, W. A. Students' ratings of qualities considered desirable in college professors. *School and Society,* 1940, *51,* 253–256.

Brandenburg, G. C., and Remmers, H. H. The Purdue Rating Scale for Instructors. *Education Administration and Supervision,* 1927, *13,* 399–406.

Brandis, R. The rehabilitation of university undergraduate teaching. *The Educational Record,* 1964, *45,* 56–63.

Braunstein, D. N. (Chair), Toward improved models of college teaching evaluation: Instructor, student, and organizational influences. Synposium presented at the American Psychological Association, Honolulu, September 1972.

Breiter, J., and Menne, J. Measuring teacher performance. Paper presented at the annual meeting of the National Council on Measurement in Education, Chicago, April 1974.

Bresler, J. B. Teaching effectiveness and government awards. *Science,* 1968, *160,* 164–167.

Bridger, J. A. Teacher evaluation with a computerized student opinionaire. *Improving College and University Teaching,* 1973, *21,* 43–45.

Bridges, C. M., Jr., Brown, B. B., Greenwood, G. E., and Ware, W. B. Analysis of College Teaching. Gainesville, Florida: Institute for Development of Human Resources, College of Education, University of Florida, no date.

Bridges, C. M., Jr., Ware, W. B., Brown, B. B., and Greenwood, G. Characteristics of best and worst college teachers. *Science Education,* 1971, *55,* 545–553.

Bryan, R. C. Student rating of teachers. *Improving College and University Teaching,* 1968, *16,* 200–202.

Burnett, C. W., and Badger, F. W. *The learning climate in the liberal arts college: An annotated bibliography.* Curriculum Series, Number 2. Charleston, West Virginia: Morris Harvey College, 1970.

Butzhamm, J., and Pfeiffer, M. G. Convergent and discriminant validity of college-level teaching dimensions. Technical Reports Number 9. Philadelphia, Pennsylvania: Psychological Laboratory, La Salle College, 1973.

Buxton, C. E., *College teaching: A psychologist's view.* New York: Harcourt Brace, 1956.

Caffrey, B. Use of multiple regression analysis and factor analysis to design a brief, objective assessment of instructor performance. Paper read at annual meeting of the Southeastern Psychological Association, New Orleans, April 1973.

Canter, F. M., and Meisels, M. Cognitive dissonance and course evaluation. *Improving College and University Teaching,* 1971, *19,* 111–113.

Carpenter, F., Van Egmond, E., and Jochem, J. Student preference of instructor types as a function of subject matter. *Science Education,* 1965, *49,* 235–238.

Carter, R. E. The effect of student characteristics on three student evaluations of university instruction. *Dissertation Abstracts International,* 1969, *30*(2–A), 486.

Cash, B. A classroom feedback system. *Improving College and University Teaching,* 1972, *20,* 291.

Cassel, R. N. A student course evaluation questionnaire. *Improving College and University Teaching,* 1971, *19,* 204–206.

Centra, J. A. Effectiveness of student feedback in modifying college instruction. *Journal of Educational Psychology,* 1973, *65,* 395–401.

Centra, J. A., and Linn, R. L. Student points of view in ratings of college instruction. Research Bulletin 73–60. Princeton, N.J.: Educational Testing Service, 1973.

Choy, C. The relationship of college teacher effectiveness to conceptual systems orientation and perceptual orientation. *Dissertation Abstracts International,* 1969, *30*(5–A), 1860–1861.

Clark, K. E., and Keller, R. J. Student ratings of college teaching. In Eckert, R. E. and Keller, R. J., eds., *A university looks at its program: Report of the University of Minnesota Bureau of Institutional Research, 1942–52.* Minneapolis: University of Minnesota Press, 1954.

Clinton, R. J. Qualities college students desire in college instructors, *School and Society,* 1930, *32,* 702.

Cohen, S. H., and Berger, W. G. Dimensions of students' ratings of college instructors underlying subsequent achievement on course examinations. *Proceedings, 78th Annual Convention, APA,* 1970, 605–606.

Comaford, C. Changes in student rating of instructor. Unpublished research paper, University of Minnesota, Department of Psychology, 1951.

Cook, W. W., and Leeds, C. H. Measuring the teaching personality. *Educational and Psychological Measurement,* 1947, *7,* 399–410.

Cope, R. G., McMillin, J. G., and Richardson, J. M. A study of the relationship between quality instruction as perceived by students and research productivity in academic departments. Seattle, Wash.: College of Education, University of Washington, 1972. Duplicated report.

Costin, F. A graduate course in the teaching of psychology: Description and evaluation. *Journal of Teaching Education,* 1968, *19,* 425–432.

Crannell, C. W. Experiment in the rating of instructors by their students. *College and University,* 1948, *23,* 5–11.

Crawford, P. L., and Bradshaw, H. L. Perception of characteristics of effective university teachers: A scaling analysis. *Educational and Psychological Measurement,* 1968, *28,* 1079–1085.

Dedrick, C. V. L. The relationship between perceptual characteristics and effective teaching at the junior college level. *Dissertation Abstracts International,* 1973, *33*(8–A), 4170–4171.

Domino, G. Interactive effects of achievement orientation and teaching style on academic achievement. *Journal of Educational Psychology,* 1971, *62,* 427–431.

Doty, B. A. Teaching method effectiveness in relation to certain student characteristics. *Journal of Educational Research,* 1967, *60,* 363–365.

Dow, D. Letter on "Research, teaching, and faculty fate." *Science,* 1971, *172,* 1082–1083.

Downie, N. M. Student evaluation of faculty. *Journal of Higher Education,* 1952, *23,* 495–496, 503.

Dwyer, F. M. Selected criteria for evaluating teacher effectiveness. *Improving College and University Teaching,* 1973, *21,* 51–52.

Ebel, K. E. The recognition and evaluation of teaching. Project to improve college teaching. American Association of University Professors, One Dupont Circle, Washington, D.C. 20036.

Elliot, C. K. Longitudinal use of student-constructed teacher evaluation form. *British Journal of Educational Psychology,* 1969, *39,* 309–313.

Elmore, P. B., and LaPoint, K. A. Sex factors in the evaluation of college instructors. Technical report 3.1–73. Carbondale, Illinois: Counseling and Testing Center, Southern Illinois University, 1973.

Elsmore, T. F. Letter on "Research, teaching, and faculty fate." *Science,* 1971, *172,* 1083.

Estrin, H. A. Effective and ineffective engineering instructors. *Improving College and University Teaching,* 1965, *13,* 137–140.

Farrar, W. E. Dimensions of faculty performance as perceived by faculty. *Dissertation Abstracts,* 1969, *29*(10a), 3458.

Feldhusen, J. F., and Starks, D. D. Bias in college students' ratings of instructors. *College Student Survey,* 1970, *4,* 6–9.

Feldman, K. A. Student assessment of teaching: A selected bibliography. *Improving College and University Teaching,* 1973, *21,* 62–63.

Field, T. W., Simkins, W. S., Browne, R. K., and Rich, P. Identifying patterns of teacher behavior from student evaluations. *Journal of Applied Psychology,* 1971, *55,* 466–469.

Finkbeiner, C. T., Lathrop, J. S., and Schuerger, J. M. Course and instructor evaluation: Some dimensions of a questionnaire. *Journal of Educational Psychology,* 1973, *64,* 159–163.

Flanagan, J. C. The critical incident technique. *Psychological Bulletin,* 1954, *51,* 327–358.

Follman, J. Modes and formats in student ratings scales of teaching effectiveness. Paper presented at the annual meeting of the National Council on Measurement in Education, Chicago, April 1974.

Fox, A. M., and Hein, D. D. Teacher perceptions in effective teaching. *Colorado Journal of Educational Research,* 1971, *10*(3), 45–49.

Foy, J. M. A note on lecturer evaluation by students. *Universities Quarterly,* 1969, *23,* 345–349.

Freehill, M. F. Authoritarian bias and evaluation of college experiences. *Improving College and University Teaching,* 1967, *15,* 18–19.

French, G. M. College students' concept of effective teaching determined by an analysis of teacher ratings. *Dissertation Abstracts,* 1957, *17,* 1380–1381.

Frey, P. W. Comparative judgment scaling of student course ratings. *American Educational Research Journal,* 1973, *10,* 149–154.

Fritz, M. F. Variability of judgment in rating of teachers by students. *Educational Administration and Supervision,* 1926, *12,* 630–634.

Gadzella, B. M. College students' views and ratings of an ideal professor. *College and University,* 1968, *44,* 89–96.

Gates, M., and Burnett, C. W. Students' perceptions of professors. *Improving College and University Teaching,* 1969, *17,* 234–236.

Gessner, P. K. Evaluation of instruction. *Science,* 1973, *180,* 566–570.

Getzels, J. W., and Jackson, P. W. The teacher's personality and characteristics. In N. L. Gage, ed., *Handbook of research on teaching.* Chicago: Rand-McNally and Co., 1963.

Gillmore, G. M. Approximating decline norms for the Illinois Course Evaluation Questionnaire by use of the normal curve. Research Report #432. Urbana, Illinois: Measurement and Research Division, Office of Instructional Resources, University of Illinois, 1972.

Gillmore, G. M. Estimates of reliability coefficients for items and subscales of the Illinois Course Evaluation Questionnaire. Research Report #341. Urbana, Illinois: Measurement and Research Division, Office of Instructional Resources, University of Illinois, 1973.

Gillmore, G. M., and Brandenburg, D. C. Would the proportion of students taking a class as a requirement affect student ratings of the course? Research Report #347. Urbana, Illinois: Measurement and Research Division, Office of Instructional Resources, University of Illinois, 1974.

Good, K. C. Similarity of student and instructor attitudes and student attitudes toward instructor. *Dissertation Abstracts International,* 1972, *32*(8–A), 4418–4419.

Good, K. C., and Good, L. R. Attitude similarity and attraction to an instructor. *Psychological Reports,* 1973, *33,* 335–337.

Gowin, D. B., and Payne, D. E. Evaluating instruction: Cross-perceptions of college students and teachers. *School Review,* 1962, *70,* 207–219.

Graham, M. H. The relationship between CEQ ratings and instructor's rank, class size, and course level. Research Report #337. Urbana, Illinois: Measurement and Research Division, Office of Instructional Resources, University of Illinois, 1972. (ERIC: EDO76147).

Grant, C. W. Faculty allocation of effort and student course evaluations. *The Journal of Educational Research,* 1971, *64,* 405–410.

Granzin, K. L., and Painter, J. J. A new explanation for students' course evaluation tendencies. *American Educational Research Journal,* 1973, *10,* 115–124.

Gray, C. E. The teaching model and evaluation of teaching performance. *Journal of Higher Education,* 1969, *40,* 636–642.

Greenwood, G. E., Bridges, C. M., Jr., Ware, W. B., and McLean, J. E. Student Evaluation of College Teaching Behaviors instrument: A factor analysis. *The Journal of Higher Education,* 1973, *44,* 596–604.

Gromisch, D. S., Bamford, J. C., Rous, S. N., Sall, S., and Rubin, S. A comparison of student and departmental chairman evaluations of teaching performance. *Journal of Medical Education,* 1972, *47,* 281–284.

Gustad, J. W. Policies and practices in faculty evaluation. *The Educational Record,* 1961, *42,* 194–211.

Gustad, J. W. Evaluation of teaching performance: Issues and possibilities. In C. B. T. Lee, ed., *Improving college teaching.* Washington, D.C.: American Council on Education, 1967.

Hall, D. T. The effect of teacher-student congruence upon student learning in college classes. *Journal of Educational Psychology,* 1970, *61,* 205–213.

Halstead, J. S. A model of research on ratings of courses and instructors. *Proceedings of the 78th Annual Convention of the American Psychological Association,* 1970, *5,* 625–626.

Hanke, J. E. Teacher and student perceptions as predictors of college teaching effectiveness. *Dissertation Abstracts International,* 1971, *31*(8–A), 3778.

Hanke, J. E., and Houston, S. R. Teacher and student perceptions as predictors of college teaching effectiveness. *College Student Journal,* 1972, *6*(1), 45–46.

Harry, J., and Goldner, N. S. The null relationship between teaching and research. *Sociology of Education,* 1972, *45,* 47–60.

Hartley, E. L., and Hogan, T. P. Some additional factors in student evaluations of courses. *American Educational Research Journal,* 1972, *9,* 241–250.

Harvey, N., and Barker, D. G. Student evaluation of teaching effectiveness. *Improving College and University Teaching,* 1970, *28,* 275–278.

Hayes, J. R. Research, teaching, and faculty fate. *Science,* 1971, *172,* 227–230.

Hayes, R. B. A way to measure classroom teaching effectiveness. *Journal of Teacher Education,* 1963, *14,* 168–176.

Hayes, R. B. A way to measure teaching. *Journal of Educational Research,* 1963, *57,* 47–50.

Hein, D. Effectiveness of teaching. *Colorado Journal of Educational Research,* 1971, *10*(2), 18–22.

Hein, L., and Moody, R. Current research on learning and teaching. *Educational Perspectives,* 1973, *12*(4), 21–26.

Heyn, D. R. Development and validation of a sociometric instructor evaluation instrument and procedure. Sherman, Texas: Austin College, 1972. Mimeographed.

Hicks, R. A. The relationship between publishing and teaching effectiveness of college professors. San Jose: San Jose State University, 1969. Mimeographed.

Hildebrand, M. How to recommend promotion for a mediocre teacher without actually lying. *Experiment and Innovation: New Directions in Education at the University of California,* 1971, *4,* 1–21.

Hildebrand, M. The character and skills of the effective professor. *Journal of Higher Education,* 1973, *44,* 41–50.

Hodgson, T. F. The general and primary factors in student evaluation of teaching ability. Seattle: University of Washington, 1958. Mimeographed.

Holmes, D. S. The relationship between expected grades and students' evaluations of their instructors. *Educational and Psychological Measurement,* 1971, *31,* 951–957.

Holmes, D. S. The teaching assessment blank: A form for the student assessment of college instructors. *Journal of Experimental Education,* 1971, *39,* 34–38.

Isaacson, R. L., McKeachie, W. J., and Milholland, J. E. Correlation of teacher personality variables and student ratings. *Journal of Educational Psychology,* 1963, *54,* 110–117.

Jandt, F. E. A new method of student evaluation of teaching. *Improving College and University Teaching,* 1973, *21,* 15–16.

Jiobu, R. M., and Pollis, C. A. Student evaluations of courses and instructors. *The American Sociologist,* 1971, *6,* 317–321.

Kane, M. T., Gillmore, G. M., and Crooks, T. J. The application of generalizability theory to course evaluation questionnaires. Paper presented at the annual meeting of the National Council on Measurement in Education, Chicago, April 1974.

Kelly, R. L. Great teachers. *Bulletin of Association of American Colleges.* 1929, *15,* 49–68.

Kennedy, W. R. The relationship of selected student characteristics to components of teacher/course evaluations among freshman English students at Kent State University. *Dissertation Abstracts International,* 1972, *32*(9–A), 5038–5039.

King, A. P. The self-concept and self-actualization of university faculty in relation to student perceptions of effective teaching. *Dissertation Abstracts International,* 1972, *32*(7–A), 3615.

Knapp, R. H., and Goodrich, H. B. *The collegiate origins of American scientists.* Chicago: University of Chicago Press, 1952.

Krupka, J. G. Report on faculty and student evaluation of Instructor Rating Questionnaire. Northampton, Pa.: Northampton County Area Community College, 1970.

Lacognata, A. A. University extension faculty and student role expectations: An empirical analysis. *Journal of Experimental Education,* 1964, *33,* 107–120.

Lancaster, O. E. Methods of faculty evaluation and development. *Engineering Education,* 1971, *62,* 95–97.

Lathrop, R. G. Unit factorial ratings by college students of courses and instructors. Chico State College, California, 1968.

Lathrop, R. G., and Richmond, C. College students' evaluation of courses and instructors. Chico State College, California, 1967.

Leftwich, W. H., and Remmers, H. H. A comparison of graphic and forced-choice ratings of teaching performance at the college and university level. Purdue University Studies in Higher Education, 1962, *92,* 3–35.

Leonard, W. M., II. Student preferences for what makes a good college teacher. *Improving College and University Teaching,* 1973, *21,* 10–13.

Longstaff, H. P. Analysis of factors conditioning learning in general psychology. *Journal of Applied Psychology,* 1932, *16*(1 & 2), 9–48, 131–166.

Lucas, J. A. Learning efficiency of students in varying environments. *The Journal of Experimental Education,* 1970, *39*(1), 63–68.

Lunney, G. H. Attitudes of senior students from a small liberal arts college concerning faculty and course evaluation. Research Report #29. Danville, Kentucky: Office of Institutional Research and Evaluation, Centre College of Kentucky, 1973.

McClelland, J. N. The effect of student evaluations of college instruction upon subsequent evaluations. *California Journal of Educational Research,* 1970, *21,* 88–95.

McDaniel, E. D., and Feldhusen, J. F. Relationships between faculty ratings and indexes of service and scholarship. *Proceedings, 78th Annual Convention, APA,* 1970, 619–620.

McGlone, E. L., and Anderson, L. J. The dimensions of teacher credibility. *The Speech Teacher,* 1973, *22,* 196–200.

McGrath, E. J. Characteristics of outstanding college teachers. *Journal of Higher Education,* 1962, *33,* 148.

McKeachie, W. J. Research on teaching at the college and university level. In N. L. Gage, ed., *Handbook of Research on Teaching,* pp. 1118–1172. Chicago: Rand-McNally and Co., 1963.

McKeachie, W. J. Student ratings of faculty. *AAUP Bulletin,* 1969, *55,* 439–444.

McKeachie, W. J. *Teaching tips. A guidebook for the beginning college teacher.* 6th ed. Lexington, Mass.: Lexington Books, D. C. Heath and Company, 1969.

McKeachie, W. J. Research on college teaching. Memo to the faculty No. 44. Ann Arbor, Michigan: The Center for Research on Learning and Teaching, 1971.

McKeachie, W. J. Student evaluations keyed to function. Paper presented at the meeting of the American Educational Research Association, Chicago, April 1972.

McKeachie, W. J., and Lin, Y. Sex differences in student response to college teachers: Teacher warmth and teacher sex. *American Educational Research Journal,* 1971, *8,* 221–226.

Magoon, J., and Bausell, R. B. Required versus elective course ratings. *College Student Journal,* 1973, *7*(1, part 1), 29–33.

Majer, K., and Stayrook, N. Reliability of college classroom course evaluations. Paper presented at the annual meeting of the National Council on Measurement in Education, Chicago, April 1974.

Maney, A. C. The authoritarianism dimension in student evaluations of faculty. *Sociology of Education,* 1959, *32,* 226–231.

Mann, W. R. Changes in the level of attitude sophistication of college students as a measure of teacher effectiveness. *Dissertation Abstracts,* 1969, *29*(8–A), 2443–2444.

Menard, T. L. An analysis of the relationship between teacher effectiveness and teacher appearance. *Dissertation Abstracts International,* 1973, *33*(7–A), 3394–3395.

Meredith, G. M. Dimensions of faculty-course evaluation. *The Journal of Psychology*, 1969, *73*, 27–32.

Michigan State University, Educational Development Program, *Student Instructional Rating System manual*. East Lansing, Michigan: Office of Evaluation Services, Michigan State University, no date.

Michigan State University, Educational Development Program. Student Instructional Rating System (SIRS) technical bulletin. East Lansing, Michigan: Office of Evaluation Services, University College, Michigan State University, no date.

Miklich, D. R. An experimental validation study of the Purdue Rating Scale for Instruction. *Educational and Psychological Measurement*, 1969, *29*, 963, 967.

Miller, R. I. *Evaluating faculty performance*. San Francisco: Jossey-Bass, 1972.

Morsh, J. E., Burgess, G. G., and Smith, P. N. Student achievement as a measure of instructor effectiveness. *Journal of Educational Psychology*, 1956, 47, 79–88.

Mueller, R. H., and Roach, P. J. What constitutes an 'ideal' professor? Durham, New Hampshire: Department of Psychology, University of New Hampshire, 1970.

Mueller, R. H., Roach, P. J., and Malone, J. A. College students' views of the characteristics of an "ideal" professor. *Psychology in the Schools*, 1971, *8*, 161–167.

Murray, H. G. Predicting student ratings of college teaching from peer ratings of personality traits. Paper presented at the annual meeting of the Midwestern Psychological Association, Chicago, May 1973.

Musella, D., and Rusch, R. Student opinion on college teaching. *Improving College and University Teaching*, 1968, *16*, 137–140.

Nelson, C. V., and Cossaart, E. R. The adaptation of the method of summated ratings using normal deviate weights to a form for student evaluation of instructors. Paper presented at the annual meeting of the American Educational Research Association, Chicago, April 1974.

Nichols, M. G. A study of the influences of selected variables involved in student evaluations of teacher effectiveness. *Dissertation Abstracts*, 1968, *28*(8–A), 2908.

Null, E. J., and Nicholson, E. W. Personal variables of students and their perception of university instructors. *College Student Journal*, 1972, *6*(1), 6–9.

Null, E. J., and Walter, J. E. Values of students and their ratings of a university professor. *College Student Journal*, 1972, *6*(4, part 1), 46–51.

Oles, H. J., and Lencoski, A. Changes in instructor self-ratings resulting from feedback from student evaluations. Paper read at annual meeting of the Southwestern Psychological Association, Dallas, April 1973.

Painter, J. J., and Granzin, K. L. Consistency theory as an explanation of students' course evaluation tendencies. *The Journal of Experimental Education,* 1972, *41*(1), 78–81.

Pambookian, H. S. The effect of feedback from students to college instructors on their teaching behavior. *Dissertation Abstracts International,* 1973, *33*(9–A), 4950.

Pambookian, H. S. Initial level of student evaluation of instruction as a source of influence on instructor change after feedback. *Journal of Educational Psychology,* 1974, *66,* 52–56.

Perkins, E. R. Relationships among empathy, genuineness, nonpossessive warmth, and college teacher effectiveness and selected characteristics. *Dissertation Abstracts International,* 1972, *32*(9–B), 5454–5455.

Permut, S. E. Cue utilization patterns in student-faculty evaluation. *The Journal of Psychology,* 1973, *83,* 41–48.

Perry, R. R. Evaluation of teaching behavior seeks to measure effectiveness. *College and University Business,* 1969, *47*(4), 18, 22.

Pfeiffer, M. G., and Rosbach, L. A. Teaching performance criterion development through scaling: Teacher-student points-of-view analysis. *Perceptual and Motor Skills,* 1969, *28,* 755–766.

Pfeiffer, M. G., Lehmann, W., and Scheidt, U. Cross-cultural scaling studies in the developemnt of probabilistic teaching performance criteria anchored to utility and time scales. Technical Reports Number 5. (Rev. ed.) Philadelphia, Pa.: Psychological Laboratory, La Salle College, 1970.

Pffeiffer, M. G., Lehmann, W., and Scheidt, U. Methodological investigation of perceived structure of college teaching across two cultures. *Perceptual and Motor Skills,* 1972, *35,* 619–626.

Plant, W. T., and Sawrey, J. M. Student ratings of psychology professors as teachers and the research involvement of the professors rated. *The Clinical Psychologist,* 1970, *23*(4), 15–16 and 19.

Price, J. R., and Magoon, A. J. Predictors of college student ratings of instructors. Paper presented at the annual meeting of the American Psychological Association, Washington, D. C., September 1971.

Pritchard, W. M. Student evaluation of college physics teaching. *Journal of Research in Science Teaching,* 1972, *9*(4), 383–384.

Pugh, R. C., and Richmond, M. G. The consistency of student ratings of instruction. Paper read at the annual convention of the National Council for Measurement in Education, Chicago, April 1974.

Quereshi, M. Y. Teaching effectiveness and research productivity. *Science,* 1968, *161,* 1160.

Quereshi, M. Y. Letter on "Teaching effectiveness and government awards." *Science,* 1968, *161,* 1160.

Quereshi, M. Y., and Widlak, F. W. Students' perception of a college teacher as a function of their sex and achievement level. *The Journal of Experimental Education,* 1973, *41*(3), 53–57.

Rees, R. D. Dimensions of students' points of view in rating college teachers. *Journal of Educational Psychology,* 1969, *60,* 476–482.

Remmers, H. H. Reliability and halo effect of high school and college students' judgments of their teachers. *Journal of Applied Psychology,* 1934, *18,* 619–631.

Remmers, H. H., and Baker, P. C. *Manual of instructions for the Purdue Rating Scale for Instructors.* Lafayette, Indiana: Purdue University Division of Educational Reference, 1952.

Remmers, R. H., and Elliott, D. N. The Indiana College and University Staff-Evaluation Program. *School and Society,* 1949, *70,* 168–171.

Remmers, H. H., Shock, N. W., and Kelley, E. L. An empirical study of the validity of the Spearman-Brown formula as applied to the Purdue Rating Scale. *Journal of Educational Psychology,* 1927, *18,* 187–195.

Remmers, H. H., and Stalnaker, J. M. Can students discriminate traits associated with success in teaching? *Journal of Applied Psychology,* 1928, *12,* 602–610.

Rezler, A. G. The influence of needs upon the student's perception of his instructor. *Journal of Educational Research,* 1965, *58,* 282–286.

Riley, J. W., Ryan, B. F., and Lifschitz, M. *The student looks at his teacher.* New Brunswick, N.J.: Rutgers University Press, 1950.

Rosenshine, B., Cohen, A., and Furst, N. Correlates of student preference ratings. *Journal of College Student Personnel,* 1973, *14,* 269–272.

Rous, S. N., Bamford, J. C., Jr., Gromisch, D., Rich, H., Rubin, S., and Sall, S. The improvement of faculty teaching through evaluation: A follow-up report. *Journal of Surgical Research,* 1973, *13,* 262–266.

Rous, S. N., Bamford, J. C., Jr., Gromisch, D., Rubin, S., and Sall, S. The improvement of faculty teaching through evaluation: A preliminary report. *Journal of Surgical Research,* 1971, *11,* 311–315.

Royce, J. D. Popularity and the teacher. *Education,* 1956, *77,* 233–237.

Ryans, D. G. Characteristics of teachers: Their description, comparison, and appraisal. Washington, D.C.: American Council on Education, 1960.

Ryans, D. G., and Wandt, E. A factor analysis of observed teacher behaviors in the secondary school: A study of criterion data. *Educational and Psychological Measurement,* 1952, *12,* 574–586.

Sartain, A. Q., and Waring, E. G. Interest in and value of college courses. *Journal of Applied Psychology,* 1944, *28,* 520–526.

Scott, C. S., and Thorne, G. Assessing faculty performance: A partially annotated bibliography. Monmouth, Oregon: Faculty Assessment Project, Teaching Research Division, Oregon State System of Higher Education, 1974. (Duplicated report)

Scott, O., Halpin, G., and Schnittjer, C. Student characteristics associated with student perceptions of college instruction. Paper presented at the annual meeting of the National Council on Measurement in Education, Chicago, April 1974.

Simpson, R. H., and Seidman, J. M. Student evaluation of teaching and learning. Washington, D.C.: American Association of Colleges for Teacher Education, 1962.

Slobin, Y., and Nichols, D. G. Student rating of teaching. *Improving College and University Teaching,* 1969, *27,* 244–248.

Smith, A. A. College teachers evaluated by students. *Sociology and Social Research,* 1944, *28,* 471–478.

Smithers, A. What do students expect of lecturers? *Universities Quarterly,* 1970, *24,* 230–236.

Smithers, A. Some factors in lecturing. *Educational Review,* 1970, *22,* 141–150.

Smock, H. R. (Chair), A plan for the comprehensive evaluation of college teaching. Symposium presented at the American Educational Research Association Convention, New Orleans, February 1973.

Solomon, D., Rosenberg, L., and Bezdek, W. E. Teacher behavior and student learning. *Journal of Educational Psychology,* 1964, *55,* 23–30.

Sorey, K. E. A study of the distinguishing personality characteristics of college faculty who are superior in regard to the teaching function. *Dissertation Abstracts,* 1968, *28*(12–A), 4816.

Spaights, E. Students appraise teachers' methods and attitudes. *Improving College and University Teaching,* 1967, *15,* 15–17.

Spencer, R. E. Judge consistency of course evaluation questionnaire ratings. Research report No. 211. University of Illinois, Office of Instructional Resources, no date.

Spencer, R. E., and Aleamoni, L. M. A student course evaluation questionnaire. *Journal of Educational Measurement,* 1970, *7,* 209–210.

Stallings, W. M., and Singhal, S. Some observations on the relationships between research productivity and student evaluations of courses and teachings. *The American Sociologist,* 1970, *5,* 141–143.

Stalnacher, J. M., and Remmers, H. H. Can students discriminate traits associated with success in teacher? *Journal of Applied Psychology,* 1928, *12,* 602–610.

Stuit, C. B., and Ebel, R. L. Instructor rating at a large state university. *College and University,* 1952, *27,* 247–254.

Swanson, R. A., and Sisson, D. J. The development, evaluation, and utilization of a departmental faculty appraisal system. *Journal of Industrial Teacher Education,* 1971, *9*(1), 64–79.

Taylor, R. E. An investigation of the relationship between psychological types in the college classroom and the student perception of the teacher and preferred teaching practices. *Dissertation Abstracts,* 1969, *29,* (8–A), 2575–2576.

Touq, M. S., and Feldhusen, J. F. The relationship between students' ratings of instructors and their participation in classroom discussion. Paper presented at the annual meeting of the National Council on Measurement in Education, New Orleans, February 1973.

Touq, M. S., Feldhusen, J. F., and Halstead, J. Criterion-referenced validity of student ratings of instructors. Paper presented at the annual meeting of the American Educational Research Association, New Orleans, February 1973.

Tuckman, B. W., and Oliver, W. F. Effectiveness of feedback to teachers as a function of source. *Journal of Educational Psychology,* 1968, *59,* 297–301.

Turner, R. L., Evans, J. H., Hale, T. A., Cairns, S. G., and Maleski, F. D. How do student characteristics affect their evaluations of instructors? *Education Bulletin, School of Education, Indiana University,* 1969, *45,* 47–97.

Tyler, R. W. The evaluation of teaching. In R. M. Cooper, ed., *The two sides of the log.* Minneapolis: University of Minnesota Press, 1958.

University of Washington, Evaluative and Counseling Service. An overview of the teaching evaluation at the University of Washington. Seattle: Evaluative and Counseling Services, University of Washington, 1973.

Usher, R., and Hanke, J. The "Third Force" in psychology and college teacher effectiveness research at the University of Northern Colorado. *Colorado Journal of Educational Research,* 1971, *10*(2), 2–9.

Van Horn, C. An analysis of the 1968 Course and Instructor Evaluation Report. Institutional Research Bulletin #2–68. Lafayette, Indiana: Measurement and Research Center, Purdue University, no date.

Very, P. S. Real and ideal characteristics of the teacher-student relationship. *Perceptual and Motor Skills,* 1968, *27,* 880–882.

Villano, M. W., Rosenstock, E. H., and Estes, C. A decade with a student course evaluation form at a major university. Paper presented at the annual meeting of the American Educational Research Association, Chicago, April 1974.

Voeks, V. W. Publications and teaching effectiveness. *Journal of Higher Education,* 1962, *33,* 212.

Walsh, G. V. One in five made us think. *Improving College and University Teaching,* 1972, *20,* 153–155.

Walter, J. E. Relationships between selected values of students and their perception of a university instructor. *Dissertation Abstracts International,* 1972, *32*(8–A), 4387.

Ward, W. D., Remmers, H. H., and Smalzreid, N. T. The training of teaching-personality by means of student ratings. *School and Society,* 1941, *53,* 189–192.

Weigel, R. G., Oetting, E. R., and Tasto, D. L. Differences in course grades and student ratings of teacher performance. *School and Society,* 1971, *99,* 60–62.

Whitlock, G. H., and Montogomery, J. R. Selection of outstanding teachers. *Improving College and University Teaching,* 1968, *16,* 197–199.

Whitlock, L. G. The dimensions of observer perceptions of teacher performance. *Dissertation Abstracts International,* 1973, *33*(8–B), 4006.

Widlack, F. W., McDaniel, E. D., and Feldhusen, J. F. Factor analysis of an instructor rating scale. Paper presented at the annual meeting of the American Educational Research Association, New Orleans, February 1973.

Williams, V. G. Some contributions of student evaluation to course revision. *Improving College and University Teaching,* 1973, *21,* 67–70.

Wilson, R. C., Dienst, E. R., and Watson, N. L. Characteristics of effective college teachers as perceived by their colleagues. *Journal of Educational Measurement,* 1973, *10,* 31–37.

Wilson, R. C., Gaff, J. G., and Bavry, J. L. Manual of information, faculty characteristics questionnaire (Experimental form I). Berkeley: Center for Research and Development in Higher Education, 1970, Mimeographed.

Wilson, W. B. Students rating teachers. *Journal of Higher Education,* 1932, *3,* 75–82.

Windle, L. (Chair), Toward improved models of college teaching evaluation: Instructor, student, and organizational influences. Symposium presented at the American Psychological Association, Honolulu, September, 1972.

Wofford, J. C. Attitudes and scholastic behavior. *The Journal of Educational Research,* 1968, *61,* 360–362.

Woolford, G. A. Teacher influence in a college of education. *Educational Research,* 1969, *11,* 148–152.

Yamamoto, K., and Dizney, H. F. College students' preferences among four types of professors. *Journal of College Student Personnel,* 1968, *9,* 259–264.

Yamamoto, K., Smallings, M. S., and Wiersma, J. Students' perceptions of eight professors in small colleges. *The Journal of Experimental Education,* 1972, *41*(1), 91–96.

Yonge, G. D., and Sassenrath, J. M. Student personality correlates of teacher ratings. *Journal of Educational Psychology,* 1968. *59,* 44–52.

Yongkittkul, C., Gillmore, G. M., and Brandenburg, D. C. Does the time of course meeting affect course ratings by students? Research Report #346. Urbana, Illinois: Measurement and Research Division, Office of Instructional Resources, University of Illinois, 1974.

Zelby, L. W. Student-faculty evaluation. *Science,* 1973, *183,* 1267–1270.

Index

About the Author

Kenneth O. Doyle, Jr., received the A.B. in 1966 from Marquette University and the Ph.D. in 1972 from the University of Minnesota. Since February 1972 he has been a research associate at the Measurement Services Center at the University of Minnesota, in charge of research and operations for the Faculty Evaluation and Testing divisions. Dr. Doyle is the author or coauthor of numerous papers on the conceptual and data aspects of faculty evaluation. In addition, he is the editor of *Interaction: Readings in Human Psychology* (D. C. Heath, 1973), and co-compiler (with Darlene Baden Arnold) of *A Scholar's Guide to Education and Psychology Journals* (Scarecrow Press, 1975).